Recollections and Reflections

"We were all taught to look up to missionaries as exemplary Christians, the ones doing what we all should do. But beyond the romance, what is it like to be a missionary? Even more intriguingly, what is it like to be the child of a missionary? Tim Reddish sympathetically but critically explores these questions in this excellent and fascinating memoir. He takes us with him to the mission fields in Nigeria where his parents served. He also provides later reflections on the impact (positive and negative) this had on himself and his faith, as well as on mission work. It's a very revealing, insightful, and thought provoking read."

—**Stuart Macdonald**, Professor of Church and Society, Knox College, University of Toronto

"*Recollections and Reflections: A Missionary Kid's African Experiences* is an exhilarating memoir that takes readers on a remarkable journey, which traverses different communities in Nigeria, especially in the northern region of the country. This memoir masterfully draws upon personal experiences while detailing missionary activities and their interactions with the sociopolitical, religious, and economic environment of Nigeria from the 1970s onward. It presents a sympathetic examination of these activities with perceptive insights that will captivate readers from start to finish."

—**Victor Ezigbo**, Professor of Theology and World Christianity, Bethel University

"Tim Reddish has penned a delightful retelling of his youthful years living in Nigeria. Included are adventures that will have you alternately laughing, crying, and holding your breath. At the end of each section, he shares reflections and interpretations which enhance the significance of his stories. He has also provided a useful summary of the pros and cons of the TCK (third culture kid) experience. His musings helped me to revisit my past and facilitated further processing and healing for me. I highly recommend this book to anyone who lived abroad at any point during their childhood."

—**Debbie Jones Warren** is a missionary kid and third culture storyteller

"In this memoir, one that is full of wonderful descriptions, Reddish brings to life—and reflects on—his years spent in rural Nigeria in the 1970s as a young boy and teenager. Born to British missionaries, he offers a personal glimpse into Nigeria's culture in the remote villages where his family lived and worked. With youthful curiosity and cultural sensitivity, he paints a vivid picture of the people, landscapes, local foods, and fauna—including the ever-present danger of scorpions and snakes—all of which remain etched in his memory. This is a captivating account of cultural exchange, personal growth, and an honest and personal reckoning of missionary endeavors in general. His insights into the missionary life reveal the duality of goodwill and the negative consequences that can accompany missionary work or foreign economic intervention. As an American, growing up in Mexico City, and now a citizen of Canada, I found this memoir brought back memories of my childhood lived in two cultures at once, with both its challenges and its richness. It is like living in limbo and in an expanded universe at the same time; an upbringing I would not change for all the money in the world."

—**Mike Maroney**, Retired Presbyterian Minister

Recollections *and* Reflections
—— A Missionary Kid's African Experiences ——

Tim Reddish

RESOURCE *Publications* · Eugene, Oregon

RECOLLECTIONS AND REFLECTIONS
A Missionary Kid's African Experiences

Copyright © 2025 Tim Reddish. All rights reserved. Except for brief quotations in critical publications or reviews, no part of this book may be reproduced in any manner without prior written permission from the publisher. Write: Permissions, Wipf and Stock Publishers, 199 W. 8th Ave., Suite 3, Eugene, OR 97401.

Resource Publications
An Imprint of Wipf and Stock Publishers
199 W. 8th Ave., Suite 3
Eugene, OR 97401

www.wipfandstock.com

PAPERBACK ISBN: 979-8-3852-5039-4
HARDCOVER ISBN: 979-8-3852-5040-0
EBOOK ISBN: 979-8-3852-5041-7

VERSION NUMBER 07/09/25

All scriptural references are from the New Revised Standard Version Bible (NRSV), copyright © 1989 National Council of the Churches of Christ in the United States of America. Used by permission. All rights reserved worldwide.

Map of SUM mission stations, *The Lightbearer* 72:2 (1976) 26. Used with permission, Amanda Angus, Communications Director, Pioneers-UK (pioneers.org.uk).

SUM Logo from the front cover of *The Lightbearer* 65:6 (1969). Used with permission, Amanda Angus, Communications Director, Pioneers-UK (pioneers.org.uk).

Aerial photograph of Hillcrest School in 1969/70 by Phyllis Wagner, *Simroots* 22:2 (2005) 2. Used with permission, Karen Keegan, ed. (simroots.org).

In loving memory of my parents
Dennis Edwin Reddish
(July 21, 1933—November 3, 2013)
Glenda Reddish, née Warriner
(December 29, 1939—August 15, 2024)

And my sister
Ruth Elizabeth Bannerman, née Reddish
(January 27, 1962—May 13, 1996)

Photographs taken at Kabwir, Nigeria. *Top*: In 1975; *bottom*: In 1977. *Middle*: from my parents' passports.

Jesus came [to his disciples] and said to them, "All authority in heaven and on earth has been given to me. Go therefore and make disciples of all nations, baptizing them in the name of the Father and of the Son and of the Holy Spirit, and teaching them to obey everything that I have commanded you. And remember, I am with you always, to the end of the age."

—Matthew 28:18–20

The church exists by mission, just as fire exists by burning. Where there is no mission there is no church.

—Emil Brunner

Mission is not just something that the church does; it is something done by the Spirit, who himself is the witness, who changes both the world and the church, who always goes before the church on its missionary journey.

—Lesslie Newbigin

Evangelization is an unpredictable process of bringing the gospel to people where they are, not where you would like them to be.... You must have the courage to go with them to a place that neither you nor they have ever been before.

—Vincent J. Donovan

Contents

Acknowledgments | ix
List of Abbreviations | xi
A Map of SUM Mission Stations in Nigeria | xii

Northeastern Nigeria | 1
Reflections: Part One | 22
Kabwir Days | 31
Reflections: Part Two | 47
Hillcrest School, Jos | 56
Reflections: Part Three | 70
Afterword | 85

Bibliography | 87
About the Author | 91
Other Books by Tim Reddish | 92

Acknowledgments

NATURALLY, A PROJECT LIKE this is a labor of love, one that requires time, and my retirement has enabled this to occur. Clearing out my mother's home provided further impetus, as in the process I discovered she had kept my childhood letters from boarding school, along with my report cards and additional 35mm slides from that time period. Those photographs supplemented my own large collection. Together they triggered memories—as every picture tells a story—and so pen was put to paper...

There is a special, enduring bond between fellow students who attended Hillcrest School in Jos, particularly among those of us who lived together as teenagers at Rock Haven; thank you for the many adventures, joys, and memories that we share. Those experiences profoundly impacted our lives, and I look back on those times with gratitude. I would also like to take this opportunity to thank all my teachers at Hillcrest and my various dorm parents both at Maxwell Hall and Rock Haven. I would say that your hopes and aspirations for me, just one of the many missionary kids in your care, have been realized—academically, spiritually, and as a person. I especially acknowledge my physics teacher, Mr. Cornelius Korhorn, the school chaplain, Rev. Harold Lang, and Rock Haven dorm parents, Harvey and Rene Fretz—each amazing and inspirational in their unique way. And there are many other influential people to thank, including my guardians, Peter and Rachel Turner, and the Shore, Black, Williams,

ACKNOWLEDGMENTS

and Viney families from the Sudan United Mission (SUM), along with the (former) mission society itself.

My father's interest in photography began as a means of communicating visually their work in Nigeria to supporters back in the UK. This hobby was spurred on by another missionary enthusiast, Keith Black, from SUM's Australian Branch. Not unsurprisingly, I followed them in this leisure pursuit. The vast majority of the photographs shown in this work were taken on (color) Kodachrome 35mm slides and are remarkably well-preserved. They were digitized using a JJC adaptor attached to a Nikon AF-S micro 40mm f2.8 lens on a Nikon D3500 SLR camera and then processed using GIMP (gimp.org).

I also want to acknowledge the whole team at Wipf and Stock, notably their managing editor, Matthew Wimer, my copyeditor, K. E., and typesetter, Calvin Jaffarian, for enabling this project to see the light of day.

Finally, but by no means least, I would like to thank my whole family for their continual love and support, especially my wife, Mary. I love you!

Enjoy the read . . .

Tim Reddish, Easter 2025

Abbreviations

BBC	British Broadcasting Corporation
CCK	Cross-Cultural Kid
CMS	Church Missionary Society
COCIN	The Church of Christ in Nations
CRC	Christian Reformed Church
CUMP	Cambridge University Mission Party
GCE	General Certificate of Education
MAF	Mission Aviation Fellowship
MBE	Member of the Order of the British Empire
MK	Missionary Kid
NRSV	New Revised Standard Version Bible translation
OBE	Officer of the Order of the British Empire
SIM	Sudan Interior Mission
SUM	Sudan United Mission
TCK	Third Culture Kid
UBC	University of British Columbia, Vancouver, Canada
UMS	United Missionary Society
VOA	Voice of America

SUDAN UNITED MISSION

A map showing the mission stations of the SUM (British branch) within central and northeastern Nigeria during the 1970s.

1

Northeastern Nigeria

It Began as a Stroll in the Gwoza Hills . . .

THE MEN RAN TOWARD us and quickly covered about twenty yards while chanting and shaking their ceremonial spears in a warrior-like manner. My father stood frozen to the spot, and my eight-year-old sister, Ruth, and I were hugging his waist in absolute terror. It would have been unwise to try to run; there was nowhere to go to anyway. It's not melodramatic to claim that it looked like we were about to die. The men stopped right in front of us, and we could see their vividly painted faces and stares of intimidation. It worked: we were petrified. I am sure Ruth and I were sobbing, and my father was probably silently praying. The men turned around and ran back and then repeated their threatening charge several more times. We knew our lives were literally in their hands.

This incident took place in 1970 among the hills rising above the township of Gwoza in northeastern Nigeria. We had taken a short hike up some foothills of the long mountain range that borders with Cameroon. Since we lived on the mission station at Gwoza, which housed a small hospital, a school, and a church, we couldn't help but see these nearby hills every day and naturally they aroused our curiosity. We knew people lived up there, since we saw them when they came down to trade their wares at the local market. We were amazed at the large, heavy loads that they—usually women—carried on their heads, and of the sure-footed agility of those who climbed up and down those hills. There were evidently trails up the hillside and we were told they were terraced at higher elevations and had long supported communities of various ethnicities. So one day we climbed up to take a look, at least as far as the stamina of an eight- and a ten-year-old could manage. We eventually reached a housing community and were surprised to find it deserted. My father could speak Hausa, the widely used market language, and hoped to greet and chat briefly with the inhabitants before we returned home. We therefore wandered a little further along the trail looking for people.

Before long we heard some wailing and then we stumbled upon a gathering of near-naked women and children in a clearing. They were dancing and chanting laments while all moving rhythmically together in a large circular motion. This was a most unusual sight, like nothing we had ever experienced—and never would again. Before we had a chance to register what we were witnessing, we were—as I just mentioned—repeatedly charged by a group of about a dozen men.

After the last charge, the men all gathered around us and my dad had an opportunity to speak with them. Tensions slowly diffused when he explained who we were (i.e., that my father was not some kind of government official) and that he was simply taking two of his children for a hike in the hills. They explained that a very important man in their community had died and this was his funeral. My dad responded by apologizing for our unintended intrusion in their moment of grief. They told him that had he come alone, they would have certainly killed him. But because he had trusted them with his own children, they let him live. After more apologies we were allowed to leave. We certainly experienced far more than we bargained for that day and realized that on any future adventure it would be wise to have a Nigerian guide.

Missionary Life in Rural Nigeria

About ten miles south of Gwoza is the village of Limankara. While my parents saw themselves primarily as missionaries, my father's practical skills were frequently put to good use in developing building programs for the broader mission society's[1] activities, including running hospitals and schools. Limankara had a small Bible school for training pastors in that part of northeast Nigeria and in 1971 my parents moved there to teach—in Hausa. (My dad traveled frequently to Gwoza using an aging short-wheelbase Land Rover to continue overseeing the building work.) The house itself needed renovation as this mission station hadn't been occupied for some time. Nevertheless, it was relatively grand and spacious, with a long south-facing veranda to shield the house from direct sunlight.

Our family's lifestyle in rural Nigeria at that time is worth relating for context. We had no electricity—instead, we used candles and kerosene lamps; we also had a small kerosene-powered refrigerator. The bulk of the cooking was done on an old cast-iron woodstove (in an external kitchen) and only supplemented by a kerosene Primus stove or a propane gas burner. There were no telephones; urgent, succinct, work-related messages were transmitted and received via a shortwave radio—powered by a 12V car battery—that served the whole mission society during a specific, brief time-window every morning. Speaking of radio: we listened to the BBC World Service and other radio stations on our battery-operated, multi-band, shortwave radio. And we extended its antenna's capabilities with a suitably orientated insulated wire strung up to a nearby tree or on the roof. Even then, reception was patchy.

We had no running water or a flush toilet; all the water was drawn by hand from the nearby well. (Water was made suitable for drinking using a gravity-fed double stainless-steel bucket system, housing two ten-inch-tall ceramic filtration candles.) The toilet resided in a ventilated outhouse and was an enclosed flat

---

1. The Sudan United Mission (SUM, British Branch) is not to be confused with the much larger Sudan Interior Mission (SIM). SUM has since morphed into Pioneers UK (pioneers.org.uk/history).

wooden bench-seat with an eight-to-ten-inch hole situated over a bucket. After you had finished, you sprinkled dry grass or straw into the bucket in a vain attempt to keep down the smell. Every day the bucket needed emptying into a deep hand-dug pit some suitable distance from the house. I recall how unnerving it was to go to the toilet at night, desperately hoping that the candle wouldn't be blown out by a sudden draft or attract too many flying insects—or worse, some kind of animal—while you were indisposed! Speaking of insects, it was vital to sleep under a mosquito net and we took Paludrine pills daily to protect ourselves from malaria.[2] And in the morning, you grabbed your slippers or shoes by the toe and tapped the heel on the ground to check that nothing had crawled into them overnight.

Like many Nigerians, we kept chickens for eggs and the occasional chicken dinner. However, unlike the locals, we kept ours enclosed in a largish space surrounded by chicken wire and fed them with ground corn saved from the previous year's harvest. This practice was widely perceived as bizarre and excessive, since everyone else's chickens simply scratched a meagre living wherever they wandered. (We let ours roam free in the early evening and they always returned home at night.) Grain-feeding our chickens meant they grew to a good size and that their eggs were large; both were envied. And while investing in chicken wire seemed pointless, when lethal fowl pests swept through the region, our chickens fared well because they were, essentially, already quarantined. Demonstrating these farming methods was an effective way of engaging the local community. (When we eventually left a particular mission station, it was our practice to donate the chicken wire and a good number of the chickens [for breeding]; both were much appreciated.) From time to time, a chicken became broody and would sit on her eggs for the required incubation period of twenty-one days. There was

---

2. On that note, our arms were pin cushions given the number of vaccinations (and booster shots) we received against tropical diseases. Many more missionaries would have died if it were not for such protection against cholera, typhoid, tetanus, smallpox, yellow fever, etc., as well as having access to penicillin and other antibiotics. (At some point while at Limankara, my sister Rachel was *very* seriously ill, probably with meningitis, and nearly died.)

always excitement among us kids as to how many would hatch and how many would eventually survive to adulthood. (Despite our precautions, the chicks were particularly vulnerable to birds of prey and snakes.) Looking after the chickens was our daily chore, one which we did willingly, especially Rachel.

Top: My youngest sister, Rachel, and her many friends at Limankara. (Notice the hills in the background.) At that time, she was fluent in two local languages (one being Hausa); in fact, English was a poor third through lack of the need to use it. *Bottom:* Rachel loved the chickens; she named them all and could readily distinguish between them. Once she eventually realized that one of her beloved friends had gone for the chop, she would refuse to eat a chicken dinner!

While at Limankara, I regularly cycled to the township early in the morning to buy fresh milk (by arrangement) from a local herdsman, who—by definition—was affluent. I would bring the milk home in plastic containers provided by my mom, who would then slowly bring the milk to the boil in order to kill off any parasites. Once cooled, we had the luxury of real milk rather than the usual reconstituted milk from powder. On one occasion I arrived early, before the cows had been milked. The farmer graciously offered me a cup of milk and, since I was hot, I gratefully accepted it. Alas, it was later discovered that I had roundworms, and I therefore had to take the appropriate medicine. My parents weren't best pleased and reminded me to politely say no in future and to always take drinking water with me.

Cycling was simply an everyday part of life.

Much of our food and goods were bought at the local weekly market, including our meat and cotton fabric (to make clothing for growing children).³ Bartering for the "right" price was expected and part of the normal lengthy process for purchasing items. If you didn't haggle, you were perceived to be a rich fool. Seasoned shoppers knew the appropriate worth of items and mutual respect was earned by steadily negotiating toward an agreed "final" price—a social process that, like African greetings, couldn't be rushed.

Meat markets were a fly-ridden, smelly section of the marketplace, and the animals were slaughtered not far away; both were places I tried to avoid. The accepted rule was that if a goat or cow was able to walk by itself to the market, it was fit enough to be eaten. Many animals were old and scrawny; their meat was correspondingly tough and had to be boiled forever (or prepared in a pressure cooker) to make it even edible in some form of stew. My mom fancied a change and bought a nice-looking piece of liver. Our houseboy put it in the wood oven to cook. A little later they opened the oven door to see the progress. To their horror, *worms* were wriggling out of the meat in a bid to escape the inevitable! Yes, the cow had been able to walk to the market, but the owner must have known it was literally on its last legs. Needless to say, the liver wasn't eaten.

A Hike to Ngoshe Sama

Our paid houseboy, Iliya, had relatives that lived in the hills to the east of Limankara. He had long wanted to visit his extended family with my father so that together they could share the gospel with them. So, my dad and I (now aged eleven), Iliya, and another Nigerian man made an expedition into the hills that was to last for at least three days. Day one was the three-thousand-foot ascent following our guides up the steep trail. We took our time, admired the views, and navigated the many terraces that enabled people to farm the hillside and live up there without the need to descend to the plain. While the climb was hard work,

---

3. My mom would then run up a loose-fitting, button-free, African-style shirt on her black, cast-iron, hand-cranked Singer sewing machine. (Our clothes were pressed with a heavy charcoal iron.)

the temperature became significantly cooler with elevation. Once at the top, the hills are undulating and are part of the Mandara mountain range that extends southward for a further hundred miles. We then made our way to a small market village and there we slept as honored guests on the floor of a round mud hut.

A scene from the small village where we rested
after the first day of our hike.

The next day we had a straightforward cross-country trip to Ngoshe Sama, where Iliya's relatives lived. Technically we crossed the border into Cameroon at some point, but such a distinction was meaningless in that environment—at least it was in those days. At one location along the narrow trail our guide spoke in an urgent whisper. I asked my dad what was said and he translated: They had seen baboons nearby and we were told to continue quietly and *not* to look at them. Baboons were the largest primates in the region, and we were traveling through their territory. They can become aggressive if they feel threatened, especially if the mothers are nursing their young. Looking directly at them is perceived as confrontational and must be avoided. As an eleven-year-old, I knew none of this. Being told *not* to look at them only resulted in me looking at them! Being so distracted, I then slipped on a damp rock and made a loud noise. The adults were annoyed with me. They pulled me to my feet, and we quickly and quietly continued on our way. Thankfully we didn't come across any hyenas or wild cats.

We eventually arrived at Iliya's relatives' home: a cluster of mud huts that were built on the rocky outcrops above the terraces. Other families lived in similar clusters in the locality, so making an extended community. Despite their surprise at seeing us, their hospitality was evident. We ate their best food, which was chicken—guts and all! Nothing was wasted. Frankly, it looked and tasted awful. But our family rule was that us children had to make a good attempt at eating whatever was put before us, lest we cause offence or seem unappreciative of their generosity. (After all, their own children were last in the pecking order for such a feast.) My parents had no such exemption. I had brought a very special treat with me: a can of Heinz baked beans. I used the can opener to take off the lid and heated it up on the campfire. It was the best meal I had on the whole trip. My dad whispered to me to leave some for him!

Hospitality was again evident as we were given our own mud hut to sleep in. The huts in the mountains were five-to-six-feet in diameter with a tall, steep thatched roof to shed the heavy rains. We were also given the best bed, a four-to-five-foot axe-hewed plank that had a large knot hole about two-thirds down its length. The plank was about eight inches wide and propped up at one end by a rock. We slept in our clothes, and I recall being quite cold; we were, after all, not used to being three thousand feet up. My dad was given the honor of sleeping on the plank, and it was important for etiquette's sake that he be seen to be using it. I was trying to sleep on the dirt floor. My dad, being six feet tall, wasn't doing well on the plank. And I wasn't coping much better on the hard, uneven floor.

Top: Catching the chicken that became our dinner.
Bottom: Me cranking the portable gramophone; Iliya is at the far right.

I whispered, "I can't sleep."
"Would you like to swap?"
So we did, but the floor was marginally better.[4]

4. As uncomfortable as that was, on a different overnight cycling trip to visit and encourage local pastors, we were again given the best bed as an honor and this generous hospitality would have been insulting to refuse. The small steel-framed bed even had a thin kapok mattress. However, the mattress was

What I hadn't appreciated was that I was the *first* white boy they had ever seen! Moreover, I had straight, sun-bleached blond hair. Word spread like wildfire across the hills and several men braved traveling during the dark to see this wonder. At various points throughout the night, we were interrupted by men entering the hut who then shone their flashlights in our faces. They felt the hair on my head and touched my skin to make sure it wasn't painted white. They were obviously amazed at what they saw and now couldn't deny the truth of the unbelievable rumors they had heard.

Breakfast over a warm campfire came as a blessed relief. The porridge-like substance was quite edible and filling. My dad spoke briefly in Hausa and Iliya translated into the local language. I contributed by turning a hand-cranked portable gramophone that played stories in some language; I have no idea what they were or who had made them.

After extended farewells, we started on our way back. We made it all the way home in one day without any further incident; downhill is so much easier than up. We had a lot to tell my mom and sisters that evening. And we were ready for a good meal, which was then followed by a very deep sleep.

An Expedition to Lake Chad

In the northeast corner of Nigeria is Lake Chad, a resource shared with Niger, Chad, and Cameroon.[5] In the early 1960s it

---

infested with bed bugs and as fresh meat we were eaten alive.

5. Lake Chad is a shallow lake whose surface area reduced by as much as 90 percent between the 1960s and 1990s. It has been estimated that about 50 percent of this decrease in the lake's size can be attributed to human water use, with the remainder attributed to shifting climate patterns. Major overgrazing in the region has resulted in a loss of vegetation, which contributes to a drier climate. Large and unsustainable irrigation projects built by Niger, Nigeria, Cameroon, and Chad have diverted water from both the lake itself and the Chari and Logone Rivers, the two main tributaries that feed the lake. In the last two decades there has been increased rainfall, which has partially swelled the size of the lake. See Rekacewicz, "Lake Chad: Almost Gone"; Pham-Duc et al., "Lake Chad Hydrology."

was approximately the size of Wales or Lake Erie. At that time there were islands, some of them made of floating vegetation, that supported communities and their animals. Dr. David Carling, MBE, (and others) had a passion for the region and a vision of a low-draft boat that was a purpose-built floating hospital—an operating theatre with dental and X-ray facilities and a clinic, to be more precise.[6] Doctors could then fly into airstrips located in permanent townships at the edge of the lake, travel by dinghy to the hospital boat, and then tour the locality, including the islands, and perform various surgeries. This was seen as a natural, if not unusual, extension of the mission hospitals and dispensaries already established by SUM in that region. Realizing this ambitious project naturally took time, nevertheless the boat—named *Albarka*, Hausa for "Blessing"—was launched on Lake Chad in late 1971. Many lives were transformed by this bold initiative. The lake, however, was already beginning to dry up and tragically this devastated the region and made the longer-term implementation of this project unsustainable.

Celebrating the launch of *Albarka* on Lake Chad in 1971.

6. This was to be a replacement for an aging boat called *Albishir*, Hausa for "Good News." See also Hamilton, *Lonely Lake*.

During our vacations from boarding school, my parents would try to plan special family excursions, such as the hike to Ngoshe Sama. Another memorable trip was to visit *Albarka* on Lake Chad in 1973. In addition to being an adventure, we were going with three specific tasks to undertake. The first was to open a new airstrip and ensure its readiness for the arrival of a Mission Aviation Fellowship (MAF) plane, scheduled for while we were there. Second, we were to replenish the medical supplies of the local dispensary. And finally, we were to test a novel, pedal-powered, shortwave radio to aid communication between the dispensary, the pilot, and medical facilities beyond—such as at Molai, but also in Niger and Chad.[7] The destination was a place across the border in Niger, Baroua—north of Mallam Fatori, and at the southern edge of the encroaching Sahara Desert. The township was not only close to the lake, but it also had a very deep artesian well (or borehole) that provided a stable supply of drinkable water.

We traveled by a long-wheelbase Land Rover along sandy tracks that purported to be the road. Some hours later, we crossed a dried-up riverbed that we were informed was the border between Nigeria and Niger. (At the next major town, probably Bosso, my parents presented our official paperwork to the authorities along with our travel plans.) As we continued along the sandy tracks, we passed through abandoned villages that indicated where the lake edge had once been; people were compelled to follow the receding water, the source of their livelihood. At that time, the cause of the lake's recession was somewhat of a mystery to us, but witnessing these eerie ghost towns made the phenomenon all too real.

As to be expected, African hospitality ensured our welcome was very warm, both figuratively and literally in this case because of the dry desert heat. My parents and our guide first met with the leaders of the township and exchanged greetings. They then explained the reasons for our visit.

---

7. My vague recollection is that this innovative two-way radio was not very effective, though I may be mistaken.

Top: Crossing the dry riverbed that marked the border between Nigeria and Niger. *Bottom:* A view of abandoned dwellings that once marked the edge of Lake Chad.

The Land Rover was soon unloaded, and the local nurse was thrilled to receive the medical supplies. The next day my father and various men from Baroua walked up and down the new airstrip built by the community. He was inspecting it to ensure no large or sharp stones were present that could potentially damage the plane's tires on landing. Then we waited . . . in the shade.

Eventually we heard the single-engine Cessna buzzing the township and looking over the landing strip from the air. Naturally, this aroused the attention of the whole town and people came running to see the plane land. Once the propeller stopped rotating, crowds swarmed around the plane; they had *never* seen anything like this before. The New Zealand pilot, David Graham, aided by my father and others, enforced a circle around the plane to protect it from the numerous well-meaning but overly curious people who—quite understandably—wanted to touch it. If folk ever wondered why on earth they were clearing this patch of land of its rocks and shrubs, well, now they knew. The pilot then took several of the most senior elders of the village to go for a short flight. They came dressed in their best togas and boarded the plane and the whole village watched on in awe as it went faster and faster down the dirt strip before finally taking off. The pilot circled around, banking steeply on both the left and right sides so the occupants could view their township and the lake from the air. A short time later the plane landed and the men deplaned—some a little wobbly on their feet from the experience, one they relived at length and could later pass on to their grandchildren. The pilot then took our family of five up for the same experience, keeping the trip short to conserve fuel for the flight home. A little later, farewells were exchanged and, before taking off, the MAF pilot again expressed his admiration for the excellent ground clearing to make this new landing strip. That evening, after taking a shower at the borehole, which was like being put under a high-pressure hose pipe, we could retell our own experiences of the eventful day.

The MAF plane taking off from the new airstrip at Baroua, Niger.

The next morning we decided to try and get a closer look at the *Albarka*, which was anchored some distance offshore. This meant a trip on an aging inflatable rubber dinghy fitted with an outboard motor. There was room for just three of us, so the first trip carried our guide, my father, and me. While we didn't have a key to look around inside the vessel, we wanted to see this floating medical facility that we had heard so much about.

We also knew that Lake Chad contained hippopotami, having been told stories of them by the local fishermen. Hippos may appear slow and cumbersome on the shore, but don't be fooled by that—in the water they are fast and agile; there they are king. And don't annoy them; when you see them, promptly turn your boat away from them and paddle swiftly away. The last thing you want is for a hippo to surface under your boat; they have jaws that can bite your leg off!

After paddling the dinghy away from the shore, the outboard motor was put in place and the starter rope pulled several times before the motor coughed into life. As we headed toward the *Albarka*, we noticed hippos surfacing in the distance. The sound of the engine had annoyed them and I hoped they were moving *away* from us . . .

Then the engine stopped. And when my dad pulled on the rope, nothing happened; the engine turned over but, regardless of the number of times he pulled, it would not start. We were drifting on the lake—I could still see the hippos . . . and I feared that they would be emboldened to come and investigate.

I panicked. I shouted, unhelpfully, at my dad: "Pull harder!" He then opened the lid to the gas tank to check it contained fuel: it did. Having replaced the cap, he pulled again and—miraculously, it seemed—the engine started, and my fears began to subside.

We proceeded toward the boat, still aware of the hippopotami surfacing in the distance. And then the engine stopped again and I went into high-anxiety mode once more. Yet again my father released the cap to the gas tank and pulled on the starter cord and this time the motor started promptly. What he had now realized—and I had not—was that as the fuel was being used up in the gas tank, it created a partial vacuum that inhibited further fuel flow. Air needed to be replenished in the tank to compensate for the fuel used. He then discovered a valve that did this automatically and the issue was solved.[8] Thankfully, the noise of the outboard motor dissuaded the hippos from coming closer.

Unfortunately, there was no easy way for us to board the *Albarka*; all we could do was circle around it at close quarters. However, the boat ride itself was memorable—even if it was the stuff of nightmares!

While Living at Molai Hospital, near Maiduguri

For a while we were stationed at Molai Hospital, about six miles from Maiduguri, the large capital city of northeastern Nigeria. The hospital also had a leprosy settlement that provided vital medical aid to its patients/clients. (Leprosy, now commonly referred to as Hansen's disease, was a stigmatizing scourge in the region and a much-needed and welcomed feature of mission hospitals.) With the appropriate antibiotics leprosy is a curable disease, but the illness can leave a person with permanent disabilities due to nerve damage. In situations where the stubby remains of the fingers and thumb are rigid or locked, there will obviously be severe limitations to manual dexterity. I remember Dr. Charles Todd applying Dr. Paul Brand's tendon transplant techniques,[9] pioneered in the 1950s at a mission hospital in India, to suitable recipients at Molai. The surgery transfers a tendon from the leg to the hand in such a way as to release the thumb, enabling the person to pinch and grip objects. If you think about that for a moment, you will recognize that it's truly life transforming. I, as a thirteen-year-old, was allowed to witness this surgery and it clearly made an impression on me.

---

8. To those familiar with outboard engines, this is obvious; but it wasn't for us.

9. See Wilson, *Ten Fingers for God*; Brand with Yancey, *Pain*.

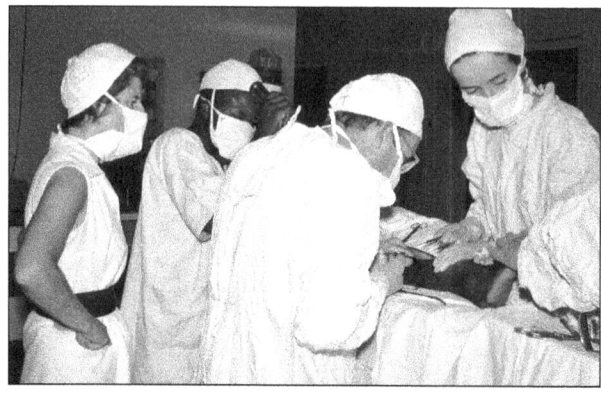

Top: A tendon transplant operation on someone suffering from the lasting effects of leprosy. *Bottom:* One of two new electricity generators being bolted to its concrete foundations.

At that time there was no electricity at the hospital and my father oversaw the installation of two Lister diesel-powered generators. They were put in a purposely designed, well-ventilated (for reasons of air-cooling) building at the edge of the hospital campus (for reasons of noise). I recall the Nigerian workmen being baffled as to why they needed to dig two large four-foot-deep rectangular holes only to fill them up again. My dad explained that the hard core and concrete were needed to provide solid, separate foundations for the two generators. Large threaded studs (adapted from a U-bolt from a truck's suspension) were embedded in the concrete, ready to firmly fix the generators to the floor. The day finally came when the delivery truck arrived with two gleaming, green generators; they only just fitted through the door.

I helped the project by going up the new poles on a ladder to attach the wires to the white ceramic pots. One day, while on the job in the early afternoon, we experienced a very significant, though partial, solar eclipse. I recall the sky went quite dark and the temperature dropped significantly. The birds went quiet, no doubt confused, thinking it was nighttime. It was certainly eerie and unsettling. I also recall that some Nigerians were quite panicked, as they didn't realize what was happening. For some it must have seemed like the end of the world—the day the sun went out.[10] Later we heard that a Concorde, filled with scientists, had been chasing the total eclipse across the Sahara Desert.[11] That was June 30, 1973. What was particularly special about this total eclipse was the *duration* of the darkness: seven minutes and four seconds, something that won't be repeated until June 25, 2150. However, traveling at Mach 2—twice the speed of sound—and at an altitude of fifty-three thousand feet, the Concorde was able to chase the eclipse, and this gave the scientists an unprecedented seventy-four minutes of darkness to perform their experiments. The terrestrial experience at Molai has been analyzed as the sun being 90 percent covered by the moon at about 1 p.m., with the most notable effects lasting over an hour.[12] Unforgettable!

At Molai, the missionaries lived about half a mile away from the hospital, separated by a straight tree-lined avenue. I was occasionally allowed to drive the mission's 50 cc moped down that road and back again. On another memorable occasion, I took my mother on the back of the moped for a spin along the road. While on

---

10. See Matt 24:29, which alludes to Isa 13:10; 34:4; Joel 2:10. (Some Christians read such texts literally and interpret them cataclysmically.)

11. See Rao, "Longest Solar Eclipses"; and Leone, "Concorde Supersonic Airliner."

12. See Time and Date, "June 30, 1973." The eclipse technically lasted for three hours.

the short ride, a ferocious sandstorm caught us out; we didn't see it coming because of the trees and we didn't hear it coming over the engine noise. As usual I was shirtless, and the sand stung my skin. We maneuvered the moped to the lee of a tree in an attempt to shelter us from the wind. My mom sat behind me to provide some protection for my bare back. We had experienced sandstorms before, but nothing of this severity and duration. I remember seeing a bird fall down dead in front of me and I was alarmed. What was the wisest thing to do? Should we wait it out or attempt to go back home? We decided to drive. It took a few attempts to pedal the engine to life in that sand-choked air, and then we turned homeward and were guided by the line of trees. Closer to our compound we were met by my father in the Land Rover coming to find us. Now that we were safe, we could admit how frightening the experience had been. We were both encrusted in sand.

This reminds me of another dramatic storm at Molai. I remember waking up one night during a tremendous thunderstorm; I lit my small kerosene bush lamp and went to investigate only to find my parents both gone. I couldn't find them anywhere—though, as I recall, I did find that my two sisters were still asleep, at least at first. Being night in a place of no electricity meant the darkness was normally only punctuated by the vivid stars and the luminous phase of the moon; but not that night, all was black . . . and the wind howled. Being raised Pentecostal, I quickly surmised that this was the rapture and I had been left behind. You may laugh, but I was *terrified*. Jesus had evidently taken all his followers away,[13] including my parents, and I was now abandoned in northern Nigeria. It didn't matter if *I* thought I was a Christian, clearly I wasn't if I was still here! Eventually my parents returned to distraught children.

The storm had ripped up a tree and hurled it on top of the nurses' quarters, whose walls were made of mud bricks, so

---

13. See Matt 24:40–44. Rapture theology was particularly popular and influential in the 1970s among conservative Christians; it still is in some circles. Being thirteen years old, I could not appreciate that apocalyptic literature was, amongst other things, a stylistic genre of warning to stir people to change their ways.

destroying the galvanized tin roof. My parents had understandably gone to investigate the crisis and see if anyone was hurt. (No injuries, mercifully, but I witnessed the seriousness of the damage the following day.) They never thought to leave an explanatory note on the table . . .

2
Reflections: Part One

Musings on the Issue of Legacy

As I reflect on the above events that occurred over fifty years ago now, I wonder about the lasting impact or legacy of my parents' work and those of other missionaries—including medical personnel and schoolteachers. It is for Nigerians themselves to fully assess and answer such questions. However, the continued existence of medical centers, such as Vom Hospital (established by Dr. Percy Barden, MBE, in 1922), Molai Hospital (established by Dr. Frances Priestman, OBE, in 1938), and Gwoza Hospital (established by Dr. Laurie Chandler, OBE, in 1956), speaks of the ongoing health needs being met within the region. Their vision and dedication, and that of many others, have evidently had an enduring legacy.

Without belittling the significance of establishing hospitals and schools, the primary aim of missionaries is arguably to spread the good news ("gospel") of Jesus Christ. In Nigeria, this has resulted in many churches being established, along with Bible schools and theological colleges to train pastors and leaders. The Sudan United Mission contributed to this endeavor for over seventy years, eventually handing over all church leadership and

REFLECTIONS: PART ONE

governance to Nigerians—to COCIN[1]—in 1977, as it should be. After all, that is the goal of mission; like the apostle Paul, missionaries then move on to new ventures in other places.

One can—and should—critique the various mission societies concerning the timings, mechanisms, and effectiveness of their hand-over processes; after all, lessons can always be learned. For example, some might argue that the transition of power, as it were, should have occurred much earlier, i.e., that the missionaries lingered too long—they didn't want to "let go." One can also critique the missionaries' underlying theological and cultural outlooks, often unconscious, that were passed on to the Nigerian church, in some cases to its detriment.[2] (I will come back to this important topic in chapter four.)

Returning to the specific region of northeastern Nigeria, where for a time my parents worked, the situation has been in utter turmoil in recent decades due to militant Sunni Islam in the form of Boko Haram.[3] This radical group seeks to introduce strict Islamic law and so wishes to overthrow the Nigerian government, which it deems is too influenced by the West. Consequently, this brutal terrorist organization is violently anti-Western, anti-Christian, and against all who it regards as collaborating with the status quo, such as security and police forces, the media, schools, politicians, and even Shia Muslims. This has obviously been devastating for countless families, since numerous people (including many non-Christians) have been killed or displaced. It has also been detrimental to churches, schools, and medical facilities in the whole of the region—including Gwoza, Limankara, greater Maiduguri, and beyond. The destructive and destabilizing influence of Boko Haram continues to impact the region to this day.

---

1. Church of Christ in Nigeria (COCIN), now renamed Church of Christ in Nations.

2. For another fascinating cultural perspective see Donovan, *Christianity Rediscovered*.

3. *Boko Haram* means "Western education is forbidden." See also Elusoji, "Twelve Years of Terror"; Mapping Militants Project, "Boko Haram"; Goitom, *Nigeria: Boko Haram*.

Various theological questions cross my mind as I reflect on this troubling turn of events, particularly in the context of divine guidance and legacy. Many evangelical Christians, like my parents, would say that God "guided" or "called" them into missionary work. Such language is consistent with the call narratives of the Old Testament prophets and is perceived as a mandate for their activities. Some readers might be surprised by such strong rhetoric, yet similar terminology is still commonly used in the ordination of Christian ministers today. In secular parlance we say someone has a "vocation," which itself is a deeply personal and empowering concept. Missionaries and ministers would likely view their work as in keeping with Jesus's parable of the sower,[4] where different soils represent various responses to the gospel. While some geographical regions and/or social conditions ("soils") are conducive to seeds growing to maturity and harvest, the parable makes it clear that this outcome is not guaranteed. The emergence and ascendancy of Boko Haram might also be linked to another farming parable of Jesus, that of the weeds.[5] In that parable, the disciples are simply encouraged to be patient, reassured that justice will eventually occur "at the end of the age," namely the Day of Judgment.[6] Many missionaries and ministers find these stories of Jesus reassuring; their job is to be faithful in the present moment, to endure, and trust in God for the eventual harvest.

Despite Paul's exhortation and reassurance in 1 Cor 15:58,[7] I still wonder though, if God knows the future, as traditional Christians maintain—could God not have been a little more strategic in implementing divine guidance to avoid such seemingly wasted

---

4. See Matt 13:1–23; Mark 4:1–20; and Luke 8:4–15.

5. See Matt 13:24–30, 36–43. This parable, unique to Matthew's Gospel, is both dualistic and apocalyptic in outlook and needs to be explored with some care and sensitivity. See also the parables in Matt 25.

6. Matt 13:27–30, 40. There is also a passivity implied here that some might find troubling.

7. "Therefore, my beloved, be steadfast, immovable, always excelling in the work of the Lord, *because you know that in the Lord your labor is not in vain*" (emphasis mine).

efforts by dedicated missionaries and aid workers?[8] In other words, is an omniscient God being efficient in maximizing the harvest? The question is obviously unanswerable, and perhaps even seen as sacrilegious in some people's minds, but it is articulated here in humility and with seriousness. The question, however, tends to depict God as a chess player, willing to sacrifice pawns to gain an overall advantage.[9] And while that analogy might be consistent with divine omnipotence, I suggest it is at odds with the true nature of divine love and the example of Jesus himself. Even so, given the self-sacrifice of some missionaries, the devastation of Boko Haram must make them—and others—wonder if it was all worth it.

Behind this question is the issue of legacy. And the very desire to have such a legacy, I suggest, points to ego and a sense of entitlement for an individual. Having said that, of course *others* may identify a person as having made a significant contribution in a certain field (e.g., politics, art, science, religion, etc.) such that they changed history in some notable way. But an individual's *ambition* to leave a legacy or receive accolades is another thing. Now, a missionary may not be consciously motivated by ambition, but as they later reflect on their life's work, they would probably hope that it made a noteworthy addition to the kingdom of God. They may be too humble to claim that for themselves, but they might like to think others with discernment would recognize their efforts as being truly worthwhile. In some cases, the missionary's activities may result in bricks and mortar—the building of a hospital or a school, for example. In other situations, it could be in establishing a vibrant church community or the training of effective leaders. In both scenarios something tangible exists that continues after

---

8. This problem arguably disappears with Open Theism because God cannot know in advance the (genuine) free choices of human beings, as that is the nature of freewill and the essence of divine love. See, for example, Sanders, *God Who Risks*; and Pinnock, *Most Moved Mover*. For a broader exploration of God's activity in a suffering world see Reddish, *Does God Always Get*.

9. In this dualistic image, who is God's chess opponent? And is an omniscient God actually responding (in real time) to his opponent's moves or is the whole game scripted—in which case it becomes something of a farce. See also Sanders and Pinnock listed in the footnote above.

the missionary has left. In the case of the areas still presently controlled by Boko Haram, the influence and activities of Christians may be extremely limited. That doesn't, however, mean it's hopeless. In the case of the suppression and persecution of the church under Communism at its height, Christianity went underground only to reemerge much later as conditions relaxed. The same outcome is possible in this situation too.

Ultimately, missionaries and ministers are faced with a decision, fundamentally one of *trust*; this is true for all of us. We are to trust *in God's providence*—in God's compassion for and activity in the world—that God's aspirations *will* be realized, and that there will eventually be a harvest even if we see no obvious signs of that at present—or even within our lifetime. Second, rather than the desire to see some tangible enduring legacy, I suggest we focus on being faithful in the moment, and to recognize that our conversations and actions may well have influenced and changed individual lives and communities in ways we may never know. In the language of the parable of the sower: we may not have personally seen much of a harvest, but we have nevertheless been sowing seed whose outcome is yet to emerge or be realized. Is that not in itself enough? Can we trust God that it is? If so, then having a palpable legacy becomes a nonissue.

The above notion is, I suggest, unsatisfactory to many Christians in the West these days. This is because there's a tendency to be seduced by the concept of church *growth*—specifically in terms of numbers and/or size of budget. Those criteria are often perceived as the mark of a "successful" church, regardless of its faithfulness to the teachings of Jesus or of evidence of profound, deep, spiritual maturity. This arises for two obvious reasons. First, they often see the harvest in the parable of the sower in purely numerical terms.[10] Perhaps this is driven by the traditional evangelical priority of simply saving *souls*. Second, which is also linked to the first, this is because the Western church has been subtly seduced by its culture, that of capitalism and commercialism. The signs of a growing company are measured in sales, profits, market share,

---

10. See also the parable of the talents, Matt 25:14–30.

size, etc., and this perspective has been uncritically imported into our understanding of church growth. Now, it's of course important to be savvy in church management, but that should also be as a result of an authentic partnership with the Holy Spirit.

Western evangelicalism, the traditional driving force behind much of Protestant missionary activity, has—in recent decades—largely bought into the above church growth model, particularly in North America. (Indeed, this attitude reinforces the notion of having an enduring legacy, because *visible* "success" itself *is* the legacy.) That being the case, the demise of a local Nigerian church that is under the oppressive thumb of Boko Haram can only be regarded as a *failure*. Personally, I do not interpret this deeply distressing matter in such stark terms, and I suspect many mission-minded churches in the West would not either. Yet there is, in my mind, a logical inconsistency here, one that needs to be candidly acknowledged by evangelicals and then authentically incorporated (or fed back) into a better understanding of church development and Christian maturity.

Moreover, this matter of legacy remains timely as many traditional church congregations in the West will close over the next two decades.[11] (In some cases, such closures may have been hastened by COVID, although the writing was probably already on the wall.) There are some congregations/denominations who will judge harshly, perhaps with an air of superiority, the theology and spirituality of those churches that close. Again, closure itself is perceived as a failure in their assumed church-growth outlook. I suggest that this attitude is not only ungracious, but that reality is far more complex—as illustrated by the above missionary example.

Some may disagree, saying that the church's decline in the West is *not* due to persecution. That's true of course. It is, however, still due to *external* cultural changes, and in that sense the two situations can be compared. In the case of Boko Haram's oppression,

---

11. That is certainly the expectation within Canada; for example, see Daly, *God Doesn't Live Here Anymore*. See also Hall, *End of Christendom*; and Clarke and Macdonald, *Leaving Christianity*.

that happened suddenly. People had to try to escape to safer regions, such as southern Nigeria or neighboring Cameroon. In contrast, the external influences on Western churches have been slow and insidious.[12] The church-growth model mentioned above is one such example; it has infected the church without her realizing it. This is not a recent issue; the church in the West has absorbed many of our culture's evolving attitudes for centuries. In one sense this is only to be expected, and those attitudes are not necessarily wrong or unhelpful. The Christian faith has been assimilated into our world's many and changing cultures from the first century onward. Indeed, Christianity—initially a small Jewish sect and then a minority religion—adapted and survived *because* of that process. It is the *uncritical* element that is key here, and to recognize that fact requires serious reflection.

The above two situations remind me of a well-known, if somewhat grotesque, analogy of a frog being placed into a jar of water. If the water is hot, the frog will recognize it as such and immediately jump out of the jar—and survive. If, however, the water is tepid, the frog will be content and remain in the jar. If the water is then slowly heated up, the frog will eventually die as, being cold-blooded, it does not realize that the temperature is increasing. In both scenarios, the external environment is involved.

In addition, many evangelical Christians would likely ascribe the church's demise in both northeastern Nigeria and in the West as due to "spiritual warfare." This dualistic outlook, also present in the New Testament, can be linked with the "God as Chess Master" metaphor, where the opponent is deemed to be Satan. Be that as it may, this situation can also be regarded as a consequence of the poor choices made *by humans*, i.e., what *we* decided to do—or *not* to do—whether consciously or unconsciously. Those decisions were obviously influenced by our upbringing, education, life-events, societal values, local circumstances, etc.[13] The present so-called culture wars in America, with the resultant polarization

---

12. See, for example, Guinness, *Gravedigger File*.

13. I suggest it is the decisions knowingly or deliberately made that are the most troubling, but that doesn't mean ignorance is bliss.

and tension in so many parts of public life, illustrate the impact of insidiously absorbed values. "Evangelicals," for example, may want to point the finger at "liberals,"[14] but what is surprising is that the supposed moral high ground of the Christian right has really become a quest for influence and power—or an endeavor to cling on to existing power—by any means possible, ethics be damned.[15] Ironically, this stance is hardly in keeping with the good news message of Jesus they claim to proclaim. What has happened to "love your enemies"?[16] To "welcoming the stranger among you"?[17] And to the "striving for unity within inevitable diversity" that Paul sought to maintain in the life of the early church?[18] When the Western church uncritically absorbs cultural values, such as non-white xenophobia, capitalism, consumerism, and nationalism, then—it seems to me—we have lost our way and need urgent reform. Numerically small churches may be doomed to close, but that does not necessarily mean large churches are inevitably "in the right" or "blessed by God." That's a gross over-simplification and another cultural lie that we have naively assumed.

In winding up these present musings, let me first say that the closing of a church *building* does not necessarily mean the end of kingdom-of-God activity in a particular location. Perhaps the building (or land) is being sold so that the money can be used for new creative ministries. As is often said, the church is *not* the building, it's the *people*. Second, perhaps we should reread and reflect upon the letters to the seven churches in the book of

---

14. I am fully aware that these over-used labels are dangerous, usually pejorative, and often ill-defined. They are generally employed as a catch-all description and with little appreciation of nuance.

15. The dangerous combination of religion, politics, and the thirst for power is not solely a feature of Boko Haram but of some Christian groups in the West, including within the USA. See, for example, Dean, *Conservatives Without Conscience*.

16. Matt 5:43–45; Luke 6:27–28; Rom 12:14, 17–19.

17. Deut 10:19; 27:19; Lev 19:33–34; 25:35; Jer 7:5–7; Zech 7:9–10; Matt 25:31–40; Luke 10:25–37.

18. For example, see Gal 3:28; Eph 4:1–6; and Rom 12; see also John 13:34–35; 15:12, 17; and 17:20–23.

Revelation.[19] There may be prophetic warnings for us to reconsider as, after all, the long-term survival of our own congregation (or denomination) is not inevitable. While some congregations have lost their first love for Jesus[20]—or are no longer salt and light, as Matthew puts it[21]—and so are slowly dying, in other cases it is failures of church leadership—of scandal, personality clashes, greed, and ego—that causes a church to split or collapse. Both scenarios are due to cultural influences that have been uncritically incorporated into the life of a church, whether conservative or liberal.

In conclusion, I repeat what I mentioned earlier: the matter of legacy is really the wrong issue or asking the wrong question. Instead, I suggest it's better to focus on *being faithful* to the cause of Christ—in partnership with the Holy Spirit—and to continue *trusting* in God's good character and in his merciful providence.

---

19. See Rev 2–3.
20. Rev 2:4.
21. Matt 5:13–16.

3
Kabwir Days

Life at the Edge of the Jos Plateau

IN LATE 1973, HAVING been in northeastern Nigeria for over three years, my parents were posted to Kabwir, southeast of the Jos plateau, which is in the center of the country. The township resides in a hilly region and is relatively temperate, given its altitude of twenty-five hundred feet. It is halfway (about ten miles) from Pankshin at four thousand feet, which essentially defines the edge of the plateau in that region, and Amper at fifteen hundred feet. While the mission station at Kabwir has a long history, being established in 1910,[1] its importance at that time was its Regional Bible School,[2] which was started in 1964. Pastors who were trained at local Bible schools, such as the one in Limankara, could train at a more advanced level at Kabwir. Furthermore, the wives of pastors could also be educated since—as in partnership—they could better serve as leaders

---

1. By the Cambridge University Mission Party (CUMP), affiliated with the Church Missionary Society (CMS). The running of the mission station was transferred to the Sudan United Mission (SUM) in 1930.

2. The Regional Bible School was (in the 1970s) as far as a pastor could train in Hausa, due to the lack of scholarly Christian books in that language. Further studies were therefore undertaken in English at the Theological College of Northern Nigeria in Bukuru; see tcnn.edu.ng.

in their local communities.[3] It was quite a financial undertaking for a pastor and his family to study at Kabwir and, if they had traveled far to be there, it involved some cultural adaptation too. My father became the principal and, with other male colleagues, taught the pastors in Hausa; my mother and other female staff taught the pastors' wives. My dad also oversaw the school's ongoing building program, which included two new teaching blocks, each containing several classrooms, and new accommodation units for the pastors and their families. My mom undertook the school's administration, including typing and duplicating all the necessary teaching materials, and keeping the financial records.

The house we lived in was the oldest on the mission compound. It was made of mud bricks with its walls rendered with mud inside and outside and then whitewashed. The aging galvanized tin roof was leaky and, rather than replace it, had thatch laid over it. The added advantage of the thatch was that it kept the interior of the house cool, aided by the house's high ceilings and many windows that enabled a through draft on a breezy day. While a thatched-roof house looks quaint—even idyllic—remember there was no electricity or running water, so things were pretty basic.

As in the rest of tropical Africa, there are only two seasons: the wet and the dry, and the rains transform the landscape from a boring brown to a lush green. Sensing when the rains are coming is important in the timing of seed planting. And the duration and dependability of the rainy season is vital for a good harvest, especially for subsistence farmers—which many people were back then—and given there were no significant mechanisms for irrigation. In that sense, everyone was—and is—in tune with nature's cycles, and sensitive to its fluctuations and longer-term changes; missionaries were no exception. The rain also clears the air, literally, in that during the height of the dry season, dust and sand particles (blown in from the Sahara—the "harmattan") stay suspended in the atmosphere. The amount of haze varies daily and

---

3. Culturally (at that time), the pastors' wives would minister to other women and children, and the pastors to other men. In addition to Bible knowledge, the wives were taught basic health care and other useful practical topics.

besides generally obscuring the view, it can seriously affect those with breathing difficulties and even suppress tree growth.[4] Having just two seasons seems very strange to those who are used to four, but it quickly becomes the new normal.[5]

Photos of my parents teaching (in Hausa) at the Regional Bible School, Kabwir, together with other images of my mom's administrative duties. (Notice the aging Gestetner duplicating machine!)

4. On one occasion the harmattan was so heavy—like a very dense fog—that everything had a weird bluish tinge due to Rayleigh scattering (i.e., blue light being preferentially scattered by the dust particles over red light).

5. And being relatively close to the equator means much smaller seasonal variations in daylight hours (and the timing of sunrise/sunset).

Top: **Our home at Kabwir.** *Bottom:* **The view from the hills behind our house. (Both pictures were taken during the dry season.)**

My parents were allotted a small plot of land not far from the house to plant seeds for their own needs. It was important to utilize it well and as part of being a good role model, *sons* were "expected" (i.e., required) to do their share in maintaining it. Near planting time, my father would arrange for an ox and plow to till the land. And depending on the timing of the onset of the rains and my school vacations, I would plant corn seed (each with two pellets of fertilizer) and/or weed near the bases of the seedlings to give them a fighting chance of reaching maturity. From my perspective, the plot of land seemed the size of a soccer field. I used a homemade Nigerian hand hoe—and had to be mindful of scorpions lingering in the soil. It was back-breaking work.

Each year we would save what looked like plump ears of corn, the best of the harvest, to use as seed for the following year.

The local corn or maize was hard, pale, and—frankly—tasteless. But when in season, we ate corn-on-the-cob every day. The excess harvest was milled and put in sacks to feed the chickens and stored; some of the sacks were donated to the students. Somehow, we acquired seed for American sweet corn and so one year we planted it—and it thrived. We now willingly ate delicious, bright yellow sweet corn, and again saved the best for next year's seed. Over time, more and more rows of sweet corn were planted, and I could literally taste the benefit of my labor. These memories come to mind whenever I read the farming parables of Jesus, those of the sower and the weeds.[6]

Snake Stories

About fifteen feet outside the back door of our house was a well that supplied all our domestic needs. One day, my mom asked me to refill our empty storage pot with water from the well.[7] This was an enjoyable task and I was happy to oblige, not least because my dad was away. There was no pulley system, you simply lowered, hand over hand, a bucket attached to a rope to the bottom of the well. When the empty bucket reached the bottom sometimes it floated. What you had to do was jerk the rope from side to side so the bucket would tip over and fill up with water. Once the bucket was full, you then began to pull it up, hand over hand, from the bottom, careful not to let it hit the sides of the well too often, otherwise lots of water would spill out.

After a while, I decided to have a rest and I looked over the rim of the well opening to see how far I'd pulled up the bucket, and how much further there was to go. As I looked down, I saw it was

---

6. See Matt 13:1–23; Mark 4:1–20; Luke 8:4–15; and Matt 13:24–30, 36–43.

7. Water was stored in a large clay pot near the kitchen door and in a forty-four-gallon steel drum raised on a concrete pedestal to gravity feed the bathroom, which housed a shallow concrete bathtub and a sink. Water was premium, not just because it was a precious commodity in itself, but because all the water was drawn by hand from the well. (All the wastewater was used to irrigate a small garden of luxury items, like tomatoes, cucumbers, etc.)

about halfway up, but to my surprise and horror I also saw a snake! It had somehow got stuck in the well and then caught up in my bucket. In a bid for freedom, it began to slither up the rope toward me. I panicked and instinctively let go of the rope. The bucket, rope, and snake all fell to the bottom of the well.

My mom came out of the house in response to my shouts. And while she understood why I'd let go, she was also annoyed because I had lost the rope and bucket, so how were we to get water now? News soon got around the village about our problem. A courageous man—probably a well-digger—came and said he would climb down to the bottom of the well and retrieve our bucket and rope. He placed his feet on the far wall of the well, and his shoulders and hands on the near side, and slowly shuffled down the sides of the well toward the bottom, *without* a safety rope.

Near the bottom he stopped and made sure he was wedged tight. Other local men at the top of the well let down a long string which the man tied to the end of the rope. (Clearly, they knew what they were doing.) The people at the top could then pull on the string until the rope was once again in their hands. This stranger rescued our bucket. He braved the dark pit of a well, with a snake at the bottom of it, so that we could have water. Amazing. Afterward, he slowly and safely shuffled his way back out again.

You may wonder, "What happened to the snake?" The men drew bucket after bucket of water, filling up many pots (and thereby draining the well) until the snake was again caught up in the bucket. Then they very quickly and deftly brought the snake and bucket up to the surface, where they promptly killed it. Problem solved.

Snakes, scorpions, and lizards are common, and you must adapt accordingly. They also provide a good source material for stories. One evening at dusk, while we kids were at boarding school, my dad saw a cobra slither under the main door of our large chicken run. He feared for the chickens' lives, but he didn't want to enter the enclosure only to become trapped against the tall chicken wire, should the snake—sensing it was cornered—then turn to attack him. He shouted for help and my mom came running with a flashlight. Most of the chickens had already entered the henhouse to roost for the night through a one-foot-square doorway. My parents were horrified when the snake slithered through the same door. They expected to hear screeching and a commotion, but there was only silence. With my mom holding the flashlight on the doorway, my father quickly entered the chicken enclosure and ran and shut and secured the small door—there could be no escape from that exit.

The henhouse was attached to an outbuilding with a vintage cast-iron woodstove that served as our rudimentary kitchen. Inside there was also a four-foot-by-two-foot door into the henhouse, which was used during the day so we could check for eggs. My dad, with an axe in one hand and a flashlight in the other, entered the outbuilding. He then told my mother to safely enter the chicken run and repeatedly thump on the closed small door, to drive the snake toward the large door opposite where he was waiting. My dad, in turn, opened that door a crack—axe at the ready. It wasn't long before just the head of the cobra emerged, at which point my dad slammed the door shut, wedging it with his foot, firmly trapping the snake between the door and its jamb. He then promptly chopped its head off while listening to the thrashing of the snake's long tail against the other side of the door. Once the serpent's nervous energy subsided and the noise stopped, he opened the door and put the tail into a bucket in the kitchen and locked everything up for the night.

Early the following morning, he unlocked the kitchen, followed by the large henhouse door, and went in to ascertain the damage. He had expected to find carnage, with many dead chickens, but to his amazement, *all* of them had survived the drama and were simply keen to get outside and get on with their day. Having taken the required evidentiary photograph, the snake was chopped up into little pieces and fed to the chickens, who squawked in delight over their luxurious, once-in-a-lifetime meal.

My dad proudly displaying the dead snake. (Notice the covered well in the near background.)

A Night in the Hills

Behind our house was a series of rock-strewn hills that we would often explore by following one of many faint trails. The boulders themselves were of all shapes and sizes, and were separated by soil, grasses, bushes, and the occasional small tree. We particularly enjoyed climbing to the top of large rock formations to get a better view of the surrounding hills and plains.

During one school vacation, my friend Derek came to stay with us for two weeks.[8] Searching for something special to do, I asked my parents if he and I could camp out overnight in the hills. (We were all vaguely aware that wild animals lived up there, though they usually hid during the day so you couldn't see them. Indeed, we had been told that about forty years earlier, there were even leopards—that is, until hunters scared them all away.) Derek and I were about seventeen years old at the time and so my request seemed safe to them. They gave us permission: it would be an adventure. So the next afternoon, around four o'clock, my dad, Derek, and I climbed up the hill and about forty-five minutes later found a level area with a spectacular view and there we set up camp. There were no tents, just camp beds and sleeping bags, because rain was not expected. We also brought some wood with us for a fire and a bit of food for dinner and breakfast, along with plenty of drinking water. Once my father knew where we were camped, he returned home.

We made a small campfire, surrounding it by rocks to contain it, and we lit it as the sun was setting. As it grew darker, the only light we had was from the fire. (Yes, we had brought flashlights, too, but we didn't want to waste the batteries.) On a clear African night, because there was no light pollution, you could see countless stars along with the Milky Way galaxy.[9] We ate some food, recounted memories, shared stories, and generally admired the view. Then we looked behind us and to our great surprise, we noticed we weren't alone. We were being watched by numerous pairs of eyes of various sizes and separations, illuminated by the firelight. It was too dark to see what kinds of animals they were, but it was certainly unnerving.

---

8. We were close friends with the Shore family, from New Zealand, not least because their children were of a similar age to us. We kids all attended Hillcrest School in Jos and lived in the same hostel, Rock Haven; see chapter 5.

9. This is most vivid in the rainy season after a storm has cleaned the air of its dust particles, much less so during the dry season.

Kabwir Regional Bible School and mission station. We camped out in the rocky hills behind our house.

On reflection, I suppose we instinctively knew that they wouldn't belong to large animals, like hyenas or baboons, because we would never have been allowed to explore the hills in daylight, let alone camp out at night. Even so, they likely belonged to monkeys of various kinds, smaller wild cats, owls, etc.

We figured that no animal would come closer because of their fear of fire. Consequently, we had to keep the fire going, and that meant searching for nearby dry twigs and dead tree branches to burn. We didn't really sleep much that night...

We heard later that our houseboy, Jan, was *horrified* to hear we were sleeping in the hills. He told my parents, "We'd never let our children do that, it's far too dangerous." But by then it was night, and any rescue party would have to wait until the next day. My parents didn't sleep much that night either, worrying about us.

Early the following morning, as soon as the sun had risen, my dad, Jan, and another man came to find us to see if we were all right. Of course we were, and—with a little bravado—we told them of our adventure. In the end everything was fine, but we were never allowed to do that again.

Road Trip!

In addition to entertaining visitors during our school vacations, we undertook road trips ourselves, often to see other missionaries. My sister Ruth had a German school friend whose parents were part of the Lutheran branch of the Sudan United Mission, and who were stationed much further south. We knew that the journey involved a ferry crossing of the River Benue, one of the two major waterways in Nigeria—the other being the mighty River Niger. We didn't really know what to expect though, as we had never traveled in that direction before, but we knew that it would involve patiently waiting in a line-up for our turn to cross.[10] We also knew the river contained crocodiles . . .

The ferry was operated by two deafening diesel-powered propellers whose direction was maneuverable and so able to steer it. You don't have any choice but to put your life in the ferry master's hands, but it was very disconcerting to pass by the sunken wreck of another ferry as we neared the other side of the river. As you drive off the ferry, you breathe a sigh of relief and then hit the road as fast as you dare to make up for lost time.

What we hadn't appreciated was that there was *another* river to cross before reaching our destination. This one was smaller, but still disturbing as this ferry was poled across the river by four or five men. We were car number four in the line-up, and we were told the ferry could only take three. To make matters worse, the sun was setting so there would be only one more crossing that day. My dad was prepared to pay the owner extra for an additional crossing, but he

---

10. This would be a hot wait since our vehicle did not have air-conditioning and we needed to conserve precious fuel.

firmly refused; it was too dangerous to traverse the river at night—he therefore wouldn't risk his livelihood for anyone.

The ferry arrived at the landing point and the vehicles disembarked. We sat in our car with the engine running, ready to move forward in the line-up, and still wondering how we could resolve our predicament. To everyone's surprise, the car in front just wouldn't start! We therefore overtook the stationary vehicle, whose hood was now up with two men frantically trying to fix the engine, and we took the final spot on the last ferry of the day.[11] When we later arrived at our hosts' mission compound, they said they never attempted the two ferry crossings in one day—it was just too unpredictable. Having crossed one river, they would stay overnight at another mission station before journeying on.

The *second* ferry of the day.

One of the things I remember most about this trip was that Ruth's friend's dad smoked a pipe. This just didn't compute for my father because, as a good Pentecostal, he maintained a strict stance of *no* smoking, drinking, dancing, swearing, movies, etc. This was an encounter he never expected: a fellow missionary smoking a

11. This might seem most uncharitable, but if we didn't overtake the car in front, someone *behind* us would then take the last spot. Naturally my parents saw this as an answer to prayer!

pipe in the privacy of his own home. This raised numerous theological questions for my father and so he proceeded to grill this Lutheran. Much later, in the car ride home, my dad blurted out to my mom: "There's no doubt about it Glenda, the man's *saved*!" Sitting silently as I was in the back of the car with my two sisters, this pronouncement amused me because why would his salvation be in doubt? He was a missionary living in the uncomfortable, humid, rainforest region of southern Nigeria—and, in my mind, that took some dedication. Was *smoking* really the "unforgiveable sin"?[12] Is it even a sin? I mean, after all, C. S. Lewis smoked a pipe!

Wase Rock

On another occasion we visited Wase (pronounced "wassey"), forty-five miles southeast of Kabwir, famed for its distinctive isolated rock—a volcanic plug—that is nearly one thousand feet tall and can be seen from up to twenty-five miles away. The place has added meaning for the Sudan United Mission because its first mission station in Nigeria was established near the rock's base in 1904. Wase had another advantage as a location: missionaries were less likely to catch debilitating—even deadly—diseases that were more prevalent in the jungle-like habitation of coastal Nigeria.[13]

A little history is in order: SUM itself began in 1904 by Dr. Karl Kumm (1874–1930), who had a love for North Africa and some knowledge of Arabic and Hausa.[14] His passion was to evangelize the Muslims in the Sudan (or "Soudan"), a broad sub-Saharan region that covered a large portion of North Africa. (Roughly speaking, this is called the Sahel today.) On August 10, 1904, four missionaries, John Burt, J. Lowry Maxwell, Dr. Ambrose Bateman, and Dr. Karl Kumm, arrived in Burutu, a port in the delta region

12. See Matt 12:31–32; Mark 3:28–29; and Luke 12:10 for mention of the unforgiveable sin "against the Holy Spirit."

13. As the well-known couplet puts it, "Beware, beware, the Bight of Benin, for few come out, though many go in."

14. See Maxwell, *Half a Century of Grace*; Tett, *Road to Freedom*; Boer, *Last of the Livingstones*.

of the River Niger. They then traveled by steamer up the river to Lokoja, where the Niger and Benue Rivers meet and, significantly, was the headquarters for the Royal Niger Company. Kumm wanted to begin work in Bauchi, northeast of Jos, but was persuaded by Sir Frederick Lugard, the British high commissioner for Northern Nigeria,[15] to start at Wase. That involved another steamship trip up the River Benue for about two hundred twenty-five miles to Ibi—another trading post—and from there, an overland trek northward of some eighty miles to Wase.

Visiting the site of the first SUM mission station at the base of Wase Rock.

On the way, John Burt developed malaria, and Dr. Bateman became seriously ill with appendicitis and had to return to Ibi—and then England. Maxwell and Burt eventually arrived at Wase nearly five weeks after leaving Ibi, and there they were reunited with Kumm, who had gone ahead to set up a base camp. They then spent several months building mud brick homes and learning Hausa. Early in 1905, they started trekking to various other

---

15. The government headquarters were at Zungeru; Kumm made the two-week round trip by boat on his own.

locations; Kumm even got as far as Bauchi. They also entertained (foreign) guests. In May 1905, Kumm returned to Europe (and later visited America) to gain further recruits, to raise funds, and, more generally, to spread his missionary vision for the region. In all three aspects he was successful. The mission station at Wase became redundant in 1909, since by then many new places (and opportunities) had been established.[16]

A Little More History...

The first of October 1960 was a momentous day in Nigeria, as that was when the country gained full independence from Britain. Not long afterward the Biafran War occurred (July 6, 1967–January 13, 1970), which has been characterized as "a political-ethnic armed conflict caused by the attempted secession of the provinces of the southeast of Nigeria, mostly populated by Igbo people."[17] Different ethnicities, aspirations, and inequalities within Nigeria, along with the discovery of oil in the southeast, fueled simmering, preexisting tensions. In January 1966, a military coup ousted the civilian government following what was deemed a fraudulent election. In July there was a countercoup by northern army units. Within a year there was civil war led by two military leaders, Lieutenant Colonels Gowan and Ojukwu, who, respectively, led the forces between Nigeria and the self-declared Republic of Biafra. Eventually Gowan won and sought to reunite the country through his famous "no victor, no vanquished" speech.[18] This was followed up with an amnesty for the majority of those who had participated in the Biafran uprising, and a noble but incomplete program of reconciliation, reconstruction, and rehabilitation. (This was remarkable for the time—and long before Nelson Mandela.) Gowan formed a fairly stable military government for five years, until he

16. The Church of Christ in Nations (COCIN) has its Karl Kumm University near Vom (Plateau State), named in honor of SUM's founder; see kku.edu.ng.

17. #Memorias Situadas, "Biafran War Memories," para. 4.

18. See Kobo, "No Victor and No Vanquished."

was forced to flee the country in July 1975 after being overthrown by another military leader in a bloodless coup.

One vacation we traveled to the southeast coast of Nigeria, the region of the Biafran Civil War. On the way we visited an Assemblies of God Bible College in Old Umuahia, roughly halfway between Enugu and Port Harcourt, and I recall seeing bullet holes—poignantly—in the large cross, made of decorative glass bricks, built into one of the buildings—a permanent physical scar of that terrible civil war. We also saw Ojukwu's bunker in Umuahia, his bolt-hole in a time of crisis. Although we came to Nigeria in 1969, because we lived in the north of the country we were shielded from the horrors of the war by distance. But we heard stories . . .

4
Reflections: Part Two

Moving Goalposts: A Changing Cultural Climate

It goes without saying that the world changed dramatically between 1904 and 1977, which was the formal duration of SUM's missionary activities in Nigeria, after which it passed the baton, as it were, to COCIN. We must also acknowledge that the Western church itself, the source of missionaries, changed significantly during that time period too—and continues to do so. The outlook of SUM's pioneering missionaries mirrored the social optimism and confidence—even triumphalism—of the late 1800s and early 1900s. Kumm therefore saw himself as bringing spiritual light into the "darkness" of the Sudan.[1] Like the rest of Europe, he was *enlightened*. Furthermore, he had a passion to *Christianize* northern Nigeria, which, from the perspective of his day, also implied bringing civilization, progress, liberty,[2] and knowledge,[3] in addi-

---

1. Boer, *Missionary Messengers*, 125. And given 1 Pet 2:9, it is no accident that the name of SUM's periodical was *The Lightbearer*, which ran from 1905 to 1991.

2. Spiritual *and* physical liberty, the latter from trans-Saharan Islamic slave traders.

3. Such as medicine and education; in the case of the latter, *who* determines the syllabus?

tion to spreading the message of salvation through Jesus Christ. This was, in the words of Jan Boer, a "paternal" attitude,[4] a term that is polite but clearly an understatement.

Enlightenment optimism collapsed, at least in Europe, with World War I and all its horrors. It was, in a sense, a war that ostensibly had Christians killing Christians, even if it was under the guise of various nationalistic flags.[5] In light of that calamitous event, the seeds of self-doubt were germinating within modernism's intelligentsia. And also within the church, for how could Europe's sending church now have the moral authority it assumed it had or, more generally, the right to see itself as contributing to bringing "civilization" and "progress" to the rest of the world?

Lamentably, within a generation the world was at war again.

After World War II, Western religious attitudes began to change—slowly at first, but gaining pace during the 1960s, for Christendom itself was ending.[6] A growing number of people no longer felt they needed church (or institutional Christianity). Consequently, fewer children were being baptized, and church attendance began to drop. No longer could a nation's identity be *assumed* to be Christian, hence the era of Christendom was over—even if its formal death came many decades later. Evangelicals were possibly the slowest to recognize or accept this cultural change. Maybe that's because they tended to view themselves as being separate from "the world." As mentioned earlier, traditional evangelicals had an emphasis on saving souls, a priority that is ultimately derived from the view that the spiritual is more important than the material, the eternal more than the temporal.[7] It's a perspec-

---

4. Boer, *Missions: Heralds of Capitalism or Christ*, 64–66. Boer stresses that paternalism is *not* to be confused with racism, and while this attitude was later abandoned in the 1920s the image of light bearer continued.

5. Many Christians forget that, theologically speaking, the kingdom of God does not recognize national boundaries.

6. See Hall, *End of Christendom*; Clarke and Macdonald, *Leaving Christianity*.

7. This is also summarized in the line from an old hymn: "This world is not my home; I'm just a passing through." Anonymous, "This World Is Not My Home."

tive that still exists in some denominations. Moreover, that attitude results in a tendency to, for example, avoid direct involvement in science, politics, the arts, and to be anti-intellectual, because those activities are generally regarded as "worldly."[8] Another reason for evangelicalism's denial was/is its persistent confidence in its view of divine providence, that "God is in control," which is in keeping with the Christian assuredness of the early 1900s. We must not forget this backdrop to the postwar missionary movement. A different, but pertinent, example is that of Lesslie Newbigin (1909–1998), who was a missionary to India from 1936 to 1974, eventually becoming the bishop of Madras. On returning to Britain he recognized that his sending church had lost confidence in the gospel. He went on to spend the rest of his life working to influence and, where possible, to rectify that demise.[9]

The above is a partial, personal, broad-brush painting of a few of the changes in the Western church and aspects of its theology during the seven decades of SUM—and beyond.[10] The key point being that missionary attitudes *evolved*, at least to some extent, over that time period. So, in assessing the merits and shortcomings of missionary activities, we cannot assume a uniform or static picture, either theologically or culturally. Neither

---

8. In the US the situation is slightly different from that of Europe and Canada. Beginning in the 1970s, a prominent conservative wing of evangelicalism became, in effect, a political lobby group seeking power and influence through the Republican Party. Despite the separation of church and state that is enshrined in the Constitution, many conservative Christians still believe the US should be a "Christian nation." The present culture wars should be appreciated in this religious context. From the perspective of the political elite, it could be argued—some might say a little cynically—that culture wars are a useful and distracting means to gain/maintain their power. From a Christian perspective however, they are really conservative evangelism's denial of the nation's changing socioreligious attitudes that are, ultimately, linked to the same factors that led to the end of Christendom in Europe and Canada. See Hall, *End of Christendom*; Clarke and Macdonald, *Leaving Christianity*; Boyd, *Myth of a Christian Nation*; and Smith et al., *45% of Americans*.

9. Some of Lesslie Newbigin's important works are *Proper Confidence*; *Gospel in a Pluralist Society*; and *Foolishness to the Greeks*.

10. This is certainly not unique to SUM, which itself was a nondenominational and multinational Christian mission.

can we ignore the diverse personalities and skill sets of the missionaries themselves. For all the above reasons, while there may arguably be a generic missionary spirit, the mindset of SUM missionaries was inevitably different in the early 1900s from, say, that of post-World War II or of post-1960, when Nigeria gained independence from Great Britain.

Some Thoughts on Christianity and Colonialism

It also goes without saying that there was inexorably a relationship between British colonial rule in Nigeria and SUM (British branch). It was a complex relationship that also changed over time for all sorts of reasons. The voice of the Nigerian church itself, especially COCIN, needs to be heard on that matter. Moreover, with my limited experience as a missionary kid, it would be foolish of me to pontificate on such a sensitive, multifaceted, and complicated topic. In these brief reflections I lean heavily on Jan Boer's astute observations, both critical and complimentary, toward SUM and—in particular—its British Branch. And for good reason, his PhD thesis (in 1979, from the Free University in Amsterdam) is remarkably well-researched and an important case study in the area of Christian mission in the context of British colonialism, and it focuses on SUM in Nigeria.[11] (Jan and Frances Boer were themselves missionaries in Nigeria with the Christian Reformed Church [CRC], closely affiliated with SUM, from 1966 to 1996.[12])

According to Boer, the British were primarily interested in West Africa not for political reasons, but rather as a source of raw materials and as a market for manufactured goods. Consequently, colonial government was established only to protect these economic interests when they were threatened.[13] The construction of

---

11. See Boer, *Missionary Messengers*; *Missions: Heralds of Capitalism or Christ?*; "Politico-Colonial Context of Missions."

12. See Boer and Boer, *Every Square Inch*.

13. In Nigeria that threat came from: (a) cutthroat competition among foreign firms within Nigeria that was creating havoc and, (b) French and German interests encroaching upon Britain's sphere of interest that were supported by

roads and railroads was therefore primarily to further that priority. (Even today a country's embassies exist throughout the world to promote—and try to protect—the nation's *own* interests, ones that are largely commercial.) In light of that historical reality, a secular definition of colonialism can be expressed in the following way:

> A country is a "colonial" country where the real dynamic is in *foreign* hands, nourished by *foreign* capital, directed by *foreign* personnel, inspired by a *foreign* spirit of enterprise, primarily directed towards *foreign* interests. A "colonial" country is therefore a country . . . of which people and land are, in the last instance, instruments and means for *foreign* purposes, and where *foreign* decisions determine these peoples' destiny.[14]

In contrast, Boer's detailed assessment of SUM concludes with what he considers to be the mission's alternate *implicit* (i.e., never stated, yet enduring) definition:

> Colonialism is a form of imperialism based on a divine mandate and designed to bring liberation—spiritual, cultural, economic, and political—by sharing the blessings of the Christ-inspired civilization of the West with a people suffering under satanic forces of oppression, ignorance, and disease, effected by a combination of political, economic, and religious forces that cooperate under a regime seeking the benefit of both ruler and ruled.[15]

That's quite a bold statement! Its obvious theological assumptions (e.g., "divine mandate," "Christ-inspired," and "satanic forces")

---

their governments. This forced the British government to provide similar protection. Boer, "Politico-Colonial Context of Missions," 168.

14. Boer, *Missionary Messengers*, 49, citing H. Kraemer, *World Cultures and World Religions*, 65; emphasis original. Boer also maintains that "in spite of certain efforts on the part of the colonial government after World War II to encourage Nigerian economic efforts, by the time of independence the economy was firmly in the hands of foreigners and the tradition of exporting raw materials and importing manufactured goods was still strong. Independence was in name only." Boer, "Politico-Colonial Context of Missions," 170.

15. Boer, *Missionary Messengers*, 218; "Politico-Colonial Context of Missions," 177.

underpin SUM's view of both colonialism *and* the Sudan. I can appreciate that Kumm and the other pioneers likely held such a view for the reasons outlined in the previous section. It also explains their paternal view as light bearers. I am not convinced missionaries of the 1960s and 1970s, including my parents, would wholeheartedly agree with that definition, but they could well have been sympathetic toward elements of it. After all, missionaries who believe that God has "called" them for such service regard themselves as fulfilling a divine mandate of sorts.

Because the above definition is based on theological assumptions, the key question is, Were the missionaries themselves consciously aware of them? Boer's earlier mention of "implicit" infers most of them were probably not. Missionaries were people committed to a cause—the cause of Christ (as they saw it)—who were willing to serve in isolated places and under austere circumstances. I suggest those missionaries were generally well-intentioned people who came from various denominations and countries, as well as from diverse socioeconomic backgrounds. Yes, looking back many decades with hindsight—especially to the post-World War II period, they should have been more critical of their inherent theological and cultural lenses or biases in their ministries.[16] I suspect, however, that such a systematic and thoughtful introspection was probably beyond the intellectual capabilities[17] of many, who were most likely preoccupied, perhaps even overwhelmed, by the numerous apparent local needs and the challenges of their day-to-day existence. Now, that doesn't mean that past missionaries and their practices should be exempt from contemporary criticism, rather their context better understood and considered. Our own faults are often the hardest to see. Nevertheless, today's mission societies and churches urgently need to better appreciate these lessons and, where necessary, change accordingly.

16. This must also include more recent Western heresies, such as the prosperity gospel and biblical inerrancy; missionaries need to be mindful not to import partisan Western controversies into their activities, especially on other continents.

17. This is *not* to say they were not well-educated; not a few were medical doctors, linguists, engineers, teachers, etc.

REFLECTIONS: PART TWO

As mentioned in the previous section, there was within some traditional missionary circles a bias against being involved in what they perceived to be secular or "worldly" activities. What other theological blind spots may also have been present? I suspect that many missionaries were theologically conservative, and that perspective was passed on to the Nigerian church—perhaps unconsciously, for the most part. Put differently, while SUM was officially nondenominational, a missionary's *own* theological perspective inevitably introduced a personal bias into their ministry. Consider, for example, the present contentious matter of the LGBTQ+ community within the church. The archbishop of Canterbury struggles to maintain unity in the worldwide Anglican communion, not least because of the large African contingent that is against full inclusion. I suspect that position is, at least in part, because of the way missionaries presented the notion of Biblical authority along with their general approach to Biblical interpretation.

In addition, Boer identifies dualism as a negative missionary legacy, meaning distinguishing between the spiritual and physical, the sacred and the secular, resulting in—as mentioned above—a withdrawing from the world (including politics) rather than being wholeheartedly engaged in it.[18] He argues that such noninvolvement, though sincere, is only self-delusion, for even a person's silence says something. (In politics, to not vote is, in fact, a "no vote.") Another aspect of this withdrawal is a lack of a systematic assessment of colonialism, capitalism, nationalism, multinational companies/monopolies, racism, etc. In other words, as already stated, the missionaries were not critical enough of their

---

18. See Boer, *Missions: Heralds of Capitalism or Christ?*, 196–205. A different, but related, kind of dualism focuses on light and darkness, good and evil, and so consequently stresses a world dominated by spiritual warfare between God and Satan. Missionaries, indeed, all Christians, naturally see themselves on God's side—as light bearers! This polarized perspective is a skewed view of what is a more complicated reality for, as Aleksandr Solzhenitsyn put it, "The line dividing good and evil cuts through the heart of every human being." *Gulag Archipelago*, 168. That being the case, the resultant, unavoidable, internal conflict is perhaps one driving force for externalizing this dichotomy, as it creates a sense of spiritual certainty and moral virtue even if it is fueled by self-deception.

own cultural, political, and theological lenses. Despite all the good that missionaries arguably did—and Kabwir Bible School still exists, Boer concludes that such weaknesses have not served the Nigerian church well in the longer term. I would add that it doesn't serve *any* church well and damages its presentation of the gospel to the wider world.

Preliminary Reflections on Types of Government and Powers of Domination

The earlier reference to the Biafran War[19] introduced an important aspect of the Nigerian political context during my time there—from 1969–1976/78.[20] From my limited experience, the notion of a military government isn't *necessarily* a bad thing, so long as stability and national unity are maintained without undue oppression. The modern Western bias that tends to automatically regard democratically elected governments as "good" and any alternative as "bad" is too simplistic.[21] For one thing, it precludes the possibility of a benevolent dictator who may gain the broad respect of the people, and who may earnestly want to hand back power to elected civilian rule and actively works toward that goal. In addition, Nigeria at that time was a young, multi-ethnic/lingual nation with bold hopes but one that had very limited experience of civilian self-governance. Indeed, postcolonial self-governance was a steep learning curve in many an African country, and the internal tensions that led to the Biafran War were not unique to Nigeria. Frictions due to ethnicity, religion, language, disparities in regional wealth and opportunities (whether real

---

19. The war also resulted in a famine that killed up to two million people.

20. I returned to the UK in 1976 to attend boarding school (for my A-levels). I visited my parents in Nigeria twice a year for two years, after which they also returned permanently to the UK; see also chapters 5 and 6.

21. American democracy, for example, has in recent years revealed its own vulnerabilities, weaknesses, and even failings due to the influence of Trumpism.

or perceived) continue even now—fifty years on.[22] Rather than simply continue to blame colonialism—or even the influence of Christian missionaries—it might be better to blame capitalism, consumerism, multinational companies and monopolies, corruption, and a general thirst for power and control. Such things are *global* and *systemic*; everyone in the world is subject to—even complicit in—such powers of domination.[23] Having said that, there are peoples and nations that are more victims than victimizers, and the lingering effects of colonialism continue to extend a long, dark shadow in many parts of the world. In African terms, Nigeria was/is a rich country with its oil, minerals, and export crops. I leave it for others, especially Nigerians themselves, to assess if their country has been able to use its wealth wisely and fairly in the sixty-five years since independence.

---

22. One could add to that list the continued presence of *foreign* influence and interference of various kinds.

23. To use theologian Walter Wink's language; see Wink, *Powers That Be*.

5
Hillcrest School, Jos

Homesick

My first memory of Nigeria is of experiencing its blast-furnace heat as our family exited the Sabena Airlines plane in Kano, the major city of the north. My second memory is of a plague of large locusts that swarmed the airport building as we waited impatiently at the long line-up for immigration. Everyone seemed oblivious to the insects, as if they were an everyday occurrence—they were not—so we bravely tried to ignore them too. Someone said, "Don't let them land on you!" At which point, my anxiety level went several notches higher as I wondered, "Why, do they *bite*?" Eventually we got our passports stamped, cleared customs with our luggage—always a nerve-racking affair at Nigerian airports in those days—and were greeted by seasoned missionaries who were expecting us, strangers in a strange land.

My parents were initially sent to the large SUM school complex at Gindiri, about fifty miles south of Jos on the plateau, where they were to undergo an intensive course to learn Hausa. It was also a time to acclimatize and adapt to the inevitable culture shock. Families were normally expected to face this experience together, but the academic term had already started. My sister Ruth and I were very naive and super-excited to begin our boarding school adventure. So, within a couple of weeks, our parents waved goodbye to us as we climbed onto the back of an open-topped truck, along with our belongings, and headed off to Hillcrest School in Jos.

My abiding memory of the next couple of weeks was of me crying; I was terribly homesick and was absolutely miserable. It was not that my classmates were unkind, although I had no one to call a real friend at that stage, it was just that I had never experienced anything like that before. It didn't help that term had already begun. I do remember that after about two weeks, my fifth-grade teacher came to see me as I sat blubbing on one of the school swings during recess. "You have to *stop* this," she said sternly. "You're not the only person here to miss their parents—and you don't see *them* crying. You need to be a good example for your younger sister."[1] So, after a few more sniffles, I did turn the emotional corner—at least in public—and tried to stop feeling sorry for myself. I had just turned ten.

In September 1969, my dorm/house parents wrote in their report to my parents: "Timothy is settling down a little slowly, but we are sure he will soon adjust himself satisfactorily." Since my house parents happened to be English, that comment should be interpreted as a typical British understatement. Nevertheless, I did settle down and began to enjoy life sharing a room (having two bunk beds) with three other boys. I have fond memories of all my school friends and house parents. In May 1970 they wrote in their report: "Your move to Gwoza[2] does not seem to have affected Timothy's happiness in the dorm at all." And in June 1970: "Throughout the school year Timothy has been an ideal boarder . . ."

---

1. Seven-year-old Ruth was in grade two and experiencing intense homesickness too.

2. Gwoza is about 450 miles from Jos. We would travel by road to Maiduguri (via Bauchi and Potiskum) and the following day on to Gwoza (via Bama). In other words, *much* further than the fifty miles to Gindiri.

A Brief History of Hillcrest School

Hillcrest School[3] was started by the Church of the Brethren Mission in 1942 with twelve students; by 1952 there were seventy. Other mission societies became interested; SUM joined in 1955 along with the Assemblies of God Mission and the United Missionary Society, and many others joined in the 1960s. It was the era of missionary *families*. By the time we arrived in 1969, there were four dorms on the school campus that housed grades one to eight,[4] named after pioneering missionaries: Studebaker (built in 1947), Livingstone (1957), Heckman (1961), and Maxwell (1961). I was in Maxwell Hall, named after SUM's J. Lowry Maxwell,[5] for boys in grades four to eight. (Part of the social adjustment was being segregated and having my sister Ruth in a different house.) This private, international, Christian school was run on North American lines, though it contained kids from other regions of the world (e.g., Australia, New Zealand, South Africa, UK, and many parts of Europe). After 1972, it also had a number of Nigerian students and day schoolers from the Jos area.[6] In those days there were about three hundred students covering all twelve grades.[7]

---

3. See Elyea, "Hillcrest School"; and "Hillcrest School, Part 2." See also www.hillcrestschool.net.

4. Although some mission societies kept all their children together in off-site hostels; more on that later.

5. See Maxwell, *Half a Century of Grace*.

6. These were often children from the broader expatriate community, even government officials.

7. For an excellent memoir see Cok, *Down Bush*.

HILLCREST SCHOOL, JOS

Center: Aerial view of Hillcrest School in 1969/70. *Top Left:* Auditorium/Chapel. *Top Right:* Newly completed junior high building. *Bottom Left:* Maxwell Hall. *Bottom Right:* High school building.

RECOLLECTIONS AND REFLECTIONS

Memories of Maxwell Hall, Swimming, and . . . Dating

For those of us students who lived on campus, our meals were prepared and served in a separate dining hall (built in 1956). I recall that our dessert was a small bowl of mixed fruit: mango, pawpaw (or papaya), guava, and other tropical fruits. Some readers may be salivating at the thought of such readily available, fresh, exotic fare. It seemed to us that we had this dessert *every* day, so much so that it became to be known as "old faithful" or "365." It was not long before I hated it, especially the smell, texture, and taste of pawpaw. I tried to pass my dessert off to those sitting next to me who were willing to have a little more. This was soon spotted and stopped by vigilant staff; we *had* to eat it, I suppose it was part of having a balanced diet. Even now, I won't eat pawpaw or mangoes, though I do miss fresh guava with its distinctive pink flesh and smell. (People often asked me what I missed about England, and I would instantly reply, *Apples!*)

As I recall, Sunday dessert was a real treat: homemade ice cream. The telltale sign was seeing one of the Nigerian cooks outside on a Saturday using a hand-cranked ice crusher. I have no recollection concerning the quality of the ice cream, but it was a very welcome luxury.

I would sometimes be teased about my English accent, and I became sensitive to other differences that singled me out—in particular, my short trousers (or pants).[8] British shorts were both short in the leg and particularly baggy—almost indecently so, and with what I called "British-style pockets" (i.e., slit or slash-style) that enabled your coins and other things to easily fall out when you sat down. (Even today, I hate such pockets with a passion.) I would *beg* my mom to seek alternative shorts, with curved jean-style pockets, from the local market or to cut the legs off old jeans that had worn out at the knees. I was also very touchy about my hair—after all, this was the seventies. In one letter home I wrote:

---

8. Using the word *trousers* singles you out as British in a North American context. In England the word *pants* means underwear! Learning the appropriate terminology is an important part of cultural adaptation.

> Something dreadful has happened; I've had my hair cut and it doesn't even go over my ears or touch my shirt collar. It looks absolutely awful—even my friends think that. So, do you think you can write a letter to Uncle Tony and Aunt Rosemary[9] saying *not* to cut my hair because I want it to grow longer . . .

Needless to say, I continued to get haircuts.

It wasn't long before I developed an American accent;[10] after all, about 85 percent of the school was North American. This seemed inevitable and unconscious on my part, though a psychologist would no doubt think differently. When we went back to England after two and a half years (for nine months), my accent softened only to become stronger again on returning to Hillcrest. In truth, I was deemed neither American nor British by citizens of those countries—either by accent or mental outlook.[11] I will return to this important topic in chapter 6.

Sometimes the desire to fit in can get you into trouble. In May 1971, nearly twelve years old, I wrote home:

> Uncle Tony will write to you concerning this, but I want to tell you now. I bought some cigarettes and was dumb enough to hide them on the school compound. A little

---

9. Our dorm parents were honorary "uncles" and "aunts"; teachers retained their formal titles of "Mr." or "Miss/Mrs."

10. This could best be described as a generic American accent, i.e., not a regional one, such as from the deep south. Even so, my accent wasn't completely American, and my British intonation—along with terminology—came through, sometimes prompting further teasing.

11. Later, when I eventually returned to England at seventeen, I managed to retain my accent for well over a year. I felt that it was an important part of my identity. It also seemed to appeal to the girls . . . A decade later, in 1987, my wife Anne and I moved to Vancouver, British Columbia, where I was a postdoctoral researcher at UBC. To my surprise, my childhood North American accent returned quickly, and I felt culturally more at home. On returning to the UK in 1988, I kept my newly found accent, though it naturally weakened with time. Since 2002 I have lived in Ontario. My family in Canada think I speak more "British" on the phone to the UK than my "normal" accent; my UK friends and family simply hear a more North American voice. Canadians, on hearing me speak, just regard me as an immigrant from the UK. Again, I appear to be in no-man's-land!

> kid found them and either somebody told him, or he was suspicious that it was us. We didn't know whether he knew or not, but we owned up anyway. Now we can't go to the canteen, no hikes without an adult present, no going out at weekends, and telling Uncle Tony when we get back from meals or asking him if we can go to school social events—like at the basketball courts. We were smoking because, you know, it is *good* to smoke once in a while with your friends . . .

Clearly, I was grounded. I can't remember if I received an additional punishment when I next saw my parents, but it wouldn't surprise me if my dad spanked me. In the next school report home, Uncle Tony wrote: "Timothy must be careful to beware of being misled by older boys."

From grade seven onward I became aware of girls, though I am not sure I was on many of *their* radars. In those days, dating was tame.[12] You simply sat together at a highly chaperoned event, such as the annual school play, or a movie in the school auditorium or outside, projected onto the white end wall of the new junior high building. If you were able to secure a *second* date then there was some hope; if not, you had been politely rejected—an experience I knew well, as I recall, though I never gave up. During high school, probably in grade ten, I once wrote home:

> Don't come up this weekend *please*. You see there is meant to be a movie night and I have a date. If you have to come to Jos, please don't upset things like you did last time. X took it well, but Y might not take it too good. Y is a short girl with long brown hair. She is fairly quiet, cute, and . . . a good Christian too. Please try to obey my proposition, she means a lot to me. If you don't, and if you do come up, I will purposefully ignore you!

Despite my optimism, I believe this was one of those one-date-only occasions. Nevertheless, I did have some steady girlfriends and, having no brothers and two younger sisters, I was generally comfortable in the company of girls.

---

12. Although some older teenagers may disagree!

One of the school hostels, Elm House,[13] had a swimming pool. The whole school loved coming to this place. In October 1974, during my grade nine year, I was so proud to pass the rigorous theory and practical exams and become a lifeguard. I recall having to rescue some formidable twelfth grade guys as part of the final test. The school's lifeguards had a weekend rota, and we took turns to watch over the pool from the top of the diving board.

Top: The joys of Elm House swimming pool. *Bottom:* Visiting the remains of the tin mines near Jos; note the large mining pond in the background.

The region around Jos was famous for its tin mines, but this boom industry that began in the early 1900s had lost much of

---

13. The hostel for the Evangelical Lutheran Mission.

its shine by the late 1960s.[14] There were—and still are—numerous abandoned opencast mine pits, slag heaps, rusting industrial equipment, and huge numbers of mining ponds containing contaminated water. It is without doubt an environmental disaster, a serious health hazard, as well as a dreadful eyesore in a picturesque region of the country. For us at that time, it was just a place to visit and explore. We clambered over the discarded equipment as if they were climbing frames on a playground. I recall the earth being an iron-rich red and the water in the large mining ponds an unnatural turquoise blue, presumably due to metal-based chemical compounds. We didn't appreciate its dangers.

On one such outing with my parents, a Nigerian boy was distressed because his goat had somehow fallen off a vertical cliff into a sizable mining pond. I volunteered to swim and rescue it, but by the time I reached the goat, it had drowned. I swam back to the entry ramp dragging it by a leg—I distinctly remember its lifeless eye staring at me—and we returned it to the lad. From an economic point of view, a goat was very valuable to his family and this loss was tragic. But at least he had the goat to back up the story he would later tell his father; no doubt the goat was cooked and eaten. It's only as I now reflect on this memory that I realize we had no idea how deep the pond was and gave no thought to its pollutants. Looking back, it wasn't the smartest thing to have done, but it probably was the wisest . . . for the sake of the boy.

More High School Memories: Rock Haven

At the end of grade eight, there was a choice to be made. The English education system was based on national Ordinary ("O") and Advanced ("A") level exams, taken when a student was typically sixteen and eighteen years old, respectively. (Good A-level grades were imperative to attend university.) Hillcrest's North

---

14. Tin put Jos on the map and caused railway lines to be linked to the city. One factor for the industry's eventual decline is thought to be the discovery of the oil in southern Nigerian during the mid-1950s—a more lucrative venture.

American-style education didn't naturally dovetail with the British GCE[15] system, so to make the academic transition less awkward, most children of British missionaries would return to the UK to attend a boarding school when they reached thirteen or fourteen years old.[16] In the 1973/74 academic year, there was a small cohort of five or six about to enter ninth grade who were expecting to leave to start their studies for their chosen O-levels, including me. The school decided to offer a pilot O-level scheme for this group. I was very keen to stay at Hillcrest and was delighted to be part of this experiment.[17] (Having lived through junior high, I was eager to experience high school.) But that meant I needed to move to an off-campus hostel, as Maxwell Hall was for grades four to eight only. Rock Haven, run by the United Missionary Society (UMS), was the perfect choice. It was a small hostel populated primarily by Canadians and it housed students from all twelve grades, so my two younger sisters could join me too. Although this meant making new friends, we were all fairly used to such changes by this time.

Rock Haven was appropriately named not only with connotations as a place for peace and rest within a Christian community, but because there was a mound of boulders that we could climb and explore, and which overlooked the compound and the city of Jos. This was our playground after school and on weekends, along with Rock Haven's aging tennis/basketball/volleyball court and a soccer pitch. That playing field was lined by a series of citrus fruit trees that kept us well supplied with grapefruit and oranges.

---

15. General Certificate of Education.

16. SUM would fly the children back to Nigeria to see their parents twice a year during UK school vacations.

17. This was an enormous staff commitment for Hillcrest at the time; I am forever grateful to those teachers and to the school's far-sighted administration. (Our syllabus/exams were through the West African Examinations Council, WAEC.) After completing my O-levels I did return to the UK for my A-levels. My one frustration was leaving Hillcrest in the middle of grade eleven and so I never got to graduate with my class (1977).

Top: **Rock Haven Dining/Study Hall.** *Bottom:* **A view of Rock Haven's dorm building, with Jos in the background.**

In grade nine I was fascinated by having a radio and picking up various international stations, such as the BBC and VOA. I was also frustrated by the poor life of my batteries. So, being creative, I found an old 12V car battery and was able to use it to power the radio. It wasn't long, however, before it was banned from my room because traces of battery acid had inadvertently got on my bedspread and ate holes in it. I can still hear the telling off I received. My radio was later supplemented by a cassette player[18] and it wasn't long before I was introduced to the music of Larry Norman . . .

18. Electrical brown outs became increasingly common in Jos due to

Despite having regular showers, I recall that I (and others) had nasty boils from time to time. I remember having one on my elbow and, on another occasion, having one on my left facial cheek. The latter one was *so* public and *so* embarrassing. It also coincided with having my tenth-grade school photograph taken. I had to turn my left cheek away from the camera, resulting in more of a side view of me rather than the normal full facial shot. I was also relieved the photos were in black and white. O vanity . . .

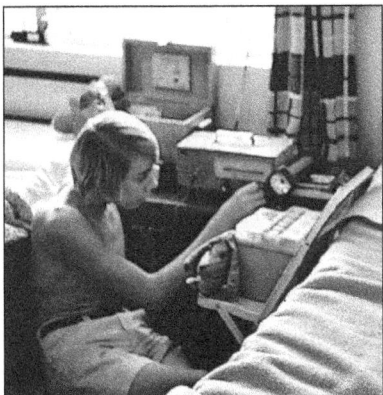 

Left: **The radio, car battery, and me!**
Right: **My grade ten yearbook picture.**

The long dorm building of Rock Haven housed the girls at one end and the boys at the other, separated by the house parents' domestic quarters and a few other rooms, including an office. The strict segregation of the two sexes' sleeping areas was thus rigorously maintained. To be fair, we were all generally well-behaved kids and didn't try to push the boundaries—though our house parents may recall things differently! We did occasionally get up to some hijinks though. I recall that one afternoon,[19] we boys

---

insufficient power being generated to meet the growing demand. Light bulbs glowed a faint brown and cassette tapes ran slow. More significantly, it played havoc with refrigerators . . .

19. It was probably during the rest hour or siesta that we routinely had at the weekends.

somehow climbed up into the attic from our end of the building and very quietly crept along the roof space toward the girls' end. I was the last boy in the train, and I gave the game away by putting my foot on an insecure timber, which then crashed through the ceiling into the office space below where there were adults present. There was a lot of shouting because the plank had narrowly missed hitting one of them. I, on the other hand, had to react quickly and grab on to the secure rafters else I would have gone through the ceiling too. The first face to sheepishly appear at the large hole was mine, and I was well and truly busted. UMS must have wondered whether it was worth having a SUM boy in their midst. Of course, *all* of us teenagers got in trouble, but there was much hilarity, too, at our audacity. I suspect this kind of mischief was nothing in comparison to that by some members of the Boy's Baptist Hostel, which had a reputation for such things . . .

A Final Word on School Rules!

Hillcrest's 1974 Student Handbook gives insight into some of the school's regulations:

1. Boys are *not* allowed to come to school in messy T-shirts and faded or ragged jeans. Hair length at maximum is to be at the base of the neck when not wearing a collar and to the base of the collar when a collar is being worn.[20] Boys are allowed to wear or grow mustaches. Sideburns should be neat and *not* below the jawbone.[21]

2. Girls may wear nice pants with matching tops. These tops come *below* the waistline so they don't have a tendency to pull up. They may wear jeans that are not faded or ragged. Tops that are worn with these jeans should be loose fitting—*no* tank tops—and should match. Dresses and skirts worn

---

20. My recollection was that the previous version of these regulations only permitted a boy's (maximum) hair length to touch the *top* of the shirt collar.
21. Clearly, growing a beard was the prerogative of male staff members.

higher than six inches above the bend of the knee will *not* be accepted.[22]

3. *No* bare feet allowed on the Hillcrest campus.
4. Gum chewing is *not* allowed in the classroom except with the teacher's permission.
5. There will be *no* smoking or drinking on the school compound or at any Hillcrest-sponsored function.

The wording of some of these rules suggests to me that lessons had been learned from trying to enforce the previous regulations!

---

22. My recollection was that the previous version of these regulations had *four* inches above the bend of the knee. The school was, I suspect, being forced to adapt to the mini skirt!

6

Reflections: Part Three

Reentry into Britain via a Very Different Boarding-School Experience

Returning to England to attend a British boarding school in Surrey was a strange reentry into what was meant to be my "home" country. You *expect* to experience culture shock when you go to *another* country, particularly one with a different language. But the widely held assumption is that on returning "home" you will instantly fit back in.[1] But I left England aged nine and returned for good at seventeen—and to a different part of the country. I was therefore experiencing a different *kind* of culture shock; I will say more about this later. Moreover, in my case, I had sun-bleached blond hair, an American accent, an unusual life story, and some overly bright clothes that were tame by African standards but inappropriate for England. The school quickly forbade me from wearing them! Unlike Hillcrest, I now had to wear a school uniform—a dull grey. And house parents were no longer referred to as "uncle" and "aunt"; instead, the house master was addressed as "sir," and we had a "matron." It all seemed so regimented and constraining,

---

1. This overlooks the fact that people's lives have moved on since you left, and that some of your previous relationships may not be recoverable.

a daily visible reminder of the pressure to conform to the expected behavior required by the school and, by extension, perhaps, UK society as a whole. Even so, it was still a coed boarding school, and I already knew how to adapt . . . and I wasn't entirely alone; there were others who were missionary kids (MKs) too, even a few from SUM who had left Nigeria at age thirteen.[2]

A little later, in 1979, Supertramp had a hit single, "The Logical Song,"[3] from their *Breakfast in America* album. The songwriter, Roger Hodgson, reportedly based the lyrics on his experience of being sent away to boarding school for ten years. I didn't appreciate that fact then. Nevertheless, this song resonated strongly with my thoughts and feelings around that time.

People sometimes ask me if I was disadvantaged academically by being educated in Nigeria. The short answer is no. At Hillcrest I was a mediocre student, though I really tried my best in high school. My strongest subjects were math, chemistry, physics, and biology, with my weakest being French and English literature. The school had an honor roll system and to be on it your grades had to be higher than B- for *all* your academic subjects.[4] This was posted on the high school bulletin board four times a term; namely, once every six weeks and the overall term grade. I *never* made the honor roll; I always had at least one C+ and sometimes worse than that. I was *so* disappointed because I had many friends who were regularly on the list. As it happened, my grades in the final six weeks of grade nine *were* all above B-. I ran to the bulletin board to proudly see my name on the list only to find it was not there. That was because I was not taking the same subjects as regular ninth grade students since I was in the O-level stream. I was crushed; I had not received any recognition

---

2. My amazing guardians, Peter and Rachel Turner, lived nearby, too, and would take me to their home for long weekends and half-terms. It really helped that they were former SUM missionaries from Nigeria with two teenagers—their son Jonathan overlapped briefly with me at Maxwell Hall.

3. For the lyrics see genius.com/Supertramp-the-logical-song-lyrics.

4. And physical education (mandatory) and choir grades had to be C- or higher.

or encouragement—the stated goal of the honor roll. And after that, I could never get higher than a C+ in French.

I believe I must have been what you might call a late developer. In the British boarding school, King Edward's School Witley (KESW),[5] I was a straight-A student.[6] Afterward I studied physics at Manchester University and graduated with first class honors. I then proceeded to graduate studies in experimental atomic and molecular physics and was awarded a PhD in 1984. So, it's fair to say I wasn't disadvantaged academically by being educated at Hillcrest. If anything, the experience taught me to be focused, determined, and it gave me a positive work ethic.

More Cultural Adjustments

I have numerous memories concerning cultural adaptation, a process that continued over many years, even decades. In 1981, my final year as an undergraduate, I had taken a girl on a date to the cinema. As I walked her home afterward along dimly lit streets, a small branch fell from an overhanging tree and landed on my head/shoulder. I abandoned her instantly and ran ahead trying to shake off the snake that I imagined had fallen off the tree on to me! That instinctive reaction provoked an amused response as I tried to explain what I was doing. It didn't ruin the date though, and the girl, Anne, eventually became my wife.

On another occasion not long afterward, I was trying to impress Anne's father, Ernest, by helping him with the gardening. He wasn't swayed when I first kicked over a rock before picking it up. He told me not to be lazy and "put my back into it." In Nigeria I was taught to *always* kick over a rock first in case there was a scorpion under it. I was sure he wouldn't believe that explanation. I had to remind myself once again: There are no scorpions in England.

---

5. See kesw.org.

6. In July 1977 I was awarded the mathematics, lower VI, and general studies prizes. In July 1978 I was awarded the physics prize.

A Traumatic Epiphany and the Start of a Journey of Self-Discovery

A few years later, in the mid-1980s, Phil, a good American friend from Rock Haven—a roommate for one year—and his wife, Gwen, came to see Anne and me (now married) in Manchester. I was thrilled to see him again after such a long time. We were hospitable and naturally took them to quintessential English places in the locality, such as Bramall Hall and Haworth, home of the Brontë sisters. What was somewhat bizarre, even disturbing, was that once they had left, I returned to our living room and *sobbed* uncontrollably for some time. Anne was deeply concerned as she had never witnessed that kind of behavior in me before. It had been a wonderful visit, so *why* was I reacting so intensely? Good question. What was going on?

I suggest my outburst was an expression of repressed grief or latent anguish, although I am not sure I could have articulated it as such at the time. A feature of my boarding school experience was repetitive cycles of friendship and loss. Missionary families returned to their home countries every two-and-a-half to three years for six to twelve months—the precise time periods depended on their mission society's policy. So each year, perhaps even each school term, some families would leave . . . and others would arrive/return. As a child you obviously had no control over the duration of your overlap with your friends. Or even if you would ever see them again in the event that they returned to their homeland for good.[7] Each one of us experienced this repetitive cycle of friendship and loss, and we coped with it in different ways. After a while, some MKs became reluctant to form new or close relationships for fear of them ending. Others, on knowing their friend would soon be leaving (or vice versa), started subconsciously to disinvest emotionally from the relationship—in order to protect their already bruised spirit—so confusing their

---

7. This could arise because a student had graduated from high school or because the parents were permanently leaving Nigeria for some other personal reason.

friend. Nevertheless, I found the bonds of friendship were generally very deep and profoundly real because we shared a common experience of living as missionary kids.

Since most of Hillcrest's missionaries were from America, my prospects of engaging with them again was effectively zero—or so I thought at the time. Remember, this was the pre-email, pre-internet era, and international telephone calls were prohibitively expensive and so not a realistic option. North America is a huge continent, so this loss was real for American and Canadian MKs too. However, in the case of large mission societies, that community still existed and periodic reunions occurred. And in some situations, it was possible for friendships to be maintained since regular communication and contact were easier. SUM (British Branch) was a relatively small outfit, and—as far as I know—its MKs simply had to fend for themselves, at least that's how it seems to me with hindsight.[8] I haven't kept in touch with any SUM MKs, although my parents were able to maintain links with other missionaries they knew, primarily through annual newsletters.[9]

On that note, it's important to recognize that adult missionaries face loss, too, when they return to their home country,[10] and so they are processing their own grief while trying to reenter society and provide for their families. That being the case, it's perhaps

---

8. If SUM had some kind of support system, I obviously fell through its cracks. Having said that, I knew my patient guardians understood me, having been SUM missionaries in Nigeria themselves.

9. Not long after my parents returned to the UK for good in 1978, I became an undergraduate at the University of Manchester. While I visited them in Scotland during some vacations, we never were a complete nuclear family again.

10. One of the losses can be one of *identity*. A home (or sending) church can be very supportive of their missionaries when they are abroad but are not sure what to do with them when they return. While abroad they were "someone," leaders even, but back home their experience and giftedness can be overlooked, perhaps even perceived to be a threat to a church's leadership, and so a former missionary can become a "nobody." Put differently, evangelical churches can easily understand and support God's original call for *sending* the missionary, but that call is sometimes perceived as a one-way ticket; does God actually call them back home at a later stage?!

not surprising if their children's emotional needs are sometimes overlooked. It's not therefore unusual for their children to rebel or, alternatively, to become introverted; either way parents are—rightly or wrongly—often blamed. I recall overtly reading David Wilkerson's[11] *I've Given Up on Parents* (1969) in the presence of company. My highly embarrassed parents could hardly complain as it was a *Christian* book!

Returning to my intense grief response: When I saw my American school friend it was a sort of resurrection; someone who was in effect dead—since he lived in the US—had come to life again, only for him to leave once more and so remind me of my broader sense of loss, perhaps even of abandonment. The visit had both elation and intense pain. In certain circumstances, to avoid the heartache it's easier to forgo the joy.

About ten years later, in May 1996, my sister Ruth died of breast cancer at the age of thirty-four. At her funeral I met up with two former SUM Hillcrest teachers who had come to pay their respects. They told me that there were school reunions in the US every three years. For some reason, I never knew. Since Anne worked for British Airways, we received company discounts so enabling me to attend the next event at Wheaton College in Illinois. While a few of my close friends couldn't be there, it was wonderful to see so many. What surprised me was that we instantly *understood* each other because of our common African/Hillcrest upbringing. Our stories of reentry—those of social and Christian (or religious) confusion—had similarities despite the obvious transatlantic differences, and this was most reassuring; I wasn't alone after all.

Christian Confusion

What do I mean by "Christian confusion," mentioned above? As well as being international, Hillcrest School and SUM were both interdenominational and that meant everyone's Christian outlooks were being broadened by that very experience. For example, I was

---

11. The famed author of *The Cross and the Switchblade*.

raised Pentecostal and a feature of that tradition in those days meant—among other banned activities—*no* movies.[12] Hillcrest organized many social activities to keep us entertained, including screening movies that were deemed suitable. Initially I was not allowed to attend them, as the school tried to accommodate, where possible, the requests of parents. However, my remaining at Maxwell Hall while all the others went to the auditorium to watch a film was singling me out as an oddity with my peers and so inhibiting my social integration. The school soon persuaded my parents to allow me to attend such events; this was a *Christian* school, after all! The point being that missionaries of different denominations/traditions learned by rubbing shoulders with each other of the authenticity of the other's faith. This was especially true for SUM by its interdenominational—even nondenominational—nature, but also for parents, through their children's experience of boarding school. As it says in Isa 11:6, "And a little child shall lead them."

Even in my mid-teen years I could appreciate the wisdom of Hillcrest's interdenominational ethos. Christians of different traditions have much more in common than that which divides us. I would add that, in the context of Christian mission, it's *totally inappropriate* to perpetuate the denominational distinctions that have arisen in (Western) church history. This understanding was, at least in part, modelled by the various mission societies themselves. Much of Nigeria was, in effect, carved up so that different missionary organizations operated in different geographical areas. In other words, they were cooperating—rather than competing—with each other, for the sake of the gospel.[13] This strikes me as broadly consistent with the early church's outlook in the New Testament. (I wonder if things are different in Nigeria now; have Western missions exported their denominationalism along with the gospel?) In short,

---

12. I recall my father being eventually persuaded by his brother, Alan, to allow us to see Disney's *Jungle Book* (released in late 1967) at the cinema, given that we were soon to be moving to Africa. We loved it, of course, but that was a special exception.

13. See map 2 in Maxwell, *Half a Century of Grace*. My perception of this cooperation may be idealized, even romanticized, as personalities and politics are to be found everywhere, but I would still like to think there is some truth to it.

living in a missionary environment, and especially my experience at Hillcrest, has broadened my Christian horizons. (I appreciate that may not be true for every MK.)

Despite my introduction to ecumenical cooperation in Nigeria, my later attendance of a British boarding school was—at first—somewhat confusing to my young faith. The Christian influence within the school was, understandably, Anglican, and that meant that in our chapel services, the chaplain wore *robes*. (A staunch Pentecostal in those days would likely consider clerical robes and stained glass windows as too close to the feared papism!) I had never seen that before; at Hillcrest, the chaplain, Rev. Harold Lang, simply wore a shirt with a collar and tie. Moreover, I grew up in a Christian subculture that was not only full of zeal but spoke its own language, often jokingly referred to as Christianese. Since these Anglicans didn't speak like that, I wasn't initially sure what to make of them. I quickly sensed the school's chaplain, Rev. John Pridmore, was a remarkable man with a big heart for all the students, and it wasn't long before I truly respected him and his wisdom. *What* he said (and *how* he acted) was far more important than the *way* he said it. This was a lesson in listening to the actual message, one with zero Christian jargon—which was, and still is, off-putting to most people anyway. It was good to have my Christian bubble burst and, again, recognize that God is still bigger.

On that note, sadly, too often when Christians disagree, we tend to fragment into yet another holy huddle—that's been the pattern in church history for centuries, at least within Protestantism. I suspect Jesus must have been aware of that tendency within his followers, given his emphasis for unity in the great pastoral prayer of John 17.[14] Many Christians are raised, and some have even lived

---

14. Jesus prays, "I ask not only on behalf of these [disciples], but also on behalf of those who will believe in me through their word, *that they may all be one*. As you, Father, are in me and I am in you, may they also be in us, so that the world may believe that you have sent me. The glory that you have given me I have given them, *so that they may be one*, as we are one, I in them and you in me, *that they may become completely one*, so that the world may know that you have sent me and have loved them even as you have loved me." John 17:20–23, emphasis mine. See also John 13:34–35; 15:12, 17.

all their lives, within the narrow confines of one denomination. I suggest that's spiritually unhealthy.[15] The world deserves a better and more unified Christian witness—if I dare use that word. It seems to me that churches in the West would do well to be more outward looking, rather than internally focused, and that could be enhanced significantly if there was greater interdenominational cooperation. Perhaps that will be the next Reformation!

Another area of confusion or challenge for me, one that's possibly more generic for missionary kids, is that of my perception of the spirituality of Christians in my homeland. As an MK, I saw that being a missionary meant 100 percent commitment and, growing up, that was what I understood to be normal for a Christian. When I returned to the UK, it didn't seem to me that many of the Christians I met had that same passion. And being young and idealistic, I judged them in my thoughts.[16] To be honest, there was/is a fair bit of nominalism about, but it took time for me to learn that there are many ways to live out a genuine Christian faith with authenticity.[17] Ways that are often more effective than an insensitive, heavy-handed approach. As St. Francis of Assisi reportedly put it, "Preach the gospel at all times, and when necessary, use words." Working in a secular environment with integrity and compassion is a noble Christian calling, too, something I tried to do in academia for over twenty-five years.

Of course, much of what I have mentioned here isn't unique to MKs; rather, it's a feature of growing in Christian maturity and

---

15. I further suggest this is one factor that fuels faith "deconstruction," an ambiguous term that is in vogue these days but, in reality, one that has a long history. Very briefly, my observation is that deconstruction often seems to replace one dogma or legalism with another, and sometimes the proverbial baby is thrown out with the bathwater. I am left wondering where is nuance—indeed, where is *faith*, since many seem to seek/prefer certainty or "proof" over faith/trust. Yes, deconstruction may well be necessary in certain situations, but so is *reconstruction*. (I have engaged in both processes on several occasions during my life.)

16. My nickname at my British boarding school was "Moses," such was my fervor perceived; make of that what you will . . .

17. See also 1 Cor 12–13.

discernment. Nevertheless, my MK experience attuned me to its importance.

On Being a "Third Culture Kid"

I met Ruth Van Reken in July 2000 at a later school reunion in Dallas. She processed her childhood MK experience much later in life, in part, by writing *Letters Never Sent* (1988) and had become something of a pioneering expert in this area of sociology.[18] Ruth led sessions at the reunion on the adaptation of MKs on returning "home" that were enormously helpful to me, and we later had several one-on-one conversations. I bought the books she recommended and devoured them.[19] They helped explain *who* I was in light of spending my formative years in Nigeria. Here is a summary of what I learned.[20]

MKs are members of what has been termed a Third Culture Kid (TCK) or, more recently, a Cross-Cultural Kid (CCK).[21] David C. Pollock defines the label in this way:

> A TCK is a person who has spent a significant part of his or her developmental years *outside* of their parents' culture. A TCK builds relationships to *all* of the cultures, while not having full ownership in any. Although elements from each culture are assimilated into the TCK's life experience, the sense of belonging is in relation to others of *similar* background.[22]

Put differently, a TCK is a "hidden immigrant" in that they may *look* like a stereotypical member of their homeland, but they *think*—and

18. See crossculturalkid.org.

19. Smith, *Strangers at Home*; Pollock and Van Reken, *Third Culture Kid Experience*.

20. This summary comes from Ruth Van Reken's presentations and papers, and from the books she recommended.

21. See, for example, Crossman, "What Is a CCK?"; and Simroots, "Resources."

22. Pollock and Van Reken, *Third Culture Kid Experience*, 19 (emphasis mine).

often *behave*—differently. TCKs include children of diplomats, military and business personnel, and others whose parents have been posted abroad, including missionaries. The degree of a person's TCK experience depends on many factors, such as the duration of their stay abroad and their degree of integration, including understanding/speaking another language. For example, those who live in a large, gated community may be more insulated from the outside culture than those who are embedded within it.

My own situation, though far from unique, was a bit more complicated. I was a British kid living in Nigeria and attending an American boarding school. I was therefore influenced by all *three* cultures, while, as Pollock puts it, "not having full ownership in any." You could perhaps say I was a *fourth* culture kid. As such, this only enhanced my degree of confusion when returning to the UK. Even so, I remain squarely under the broad umbrella of a TCK (or CCK) or as a "stranger at home."

Here are some of the now well-recognized characteristics of a TCK, the downside first:

1. Socially "backward" or off balance due to missed history while away, (e.g., music, movies, politics, and books), an inability to appreciate jokes,[23] and confusion concerning expected norms or rules (e.g., dress code or fashion, dating etiquette, and shopping/driving experience[24]).
2. Identity crisis—who else is like me?
3. Loneliness—who understands me?
4. Rootlessness—where do I fit in? (TCKs have often experienced a life of high mobility.)

---

23. In my later interactions with international academic colleagues, I discovered that humor is prone to being misunderstood because it is so rooted in a particular culture and language. This misinterpretation has the propensity to offend, something many appreciate today because emails and texting do not communicate the tone intended by the sender.

24. I recall one unusual incident in the high street: my young sister Rachel had never seen a mannequin in a store window and stood staring at it—to the surprise of onlookers—until my parents eventually dragged her away.

5. Unresolved grief, not just from past losses but from having to put on a brave face.[25]
6. A lower self-image.
7. Insecurity in relationships/commitment due to their previous cycles of deep friendships followed by irretrievable loss.
8. All the above can result in withdrawal, or anger, or depression, or paralyzing perfectionism, or heightened anxiety, or a denial of appropriate feelings, or a crisis of faith.

Taken all together, this list sounds deeply concerning and implies every TCK needs a good therapist! First, not every TCK experiences all of these characteristics, or their experiences of them are only mild and soon pass. Much depends on the support a person gets when reentering their "home" country, particularly from family and friends, but also the broader community, including their employer (e.g., mission society), school/college, church, etc. Second, some of the items, like the first one, are short-term. For example, I recall having recently returned to England and visiting my uncle and aunt in Lincolnshire. Early in the evening we were watching *Top of the Pops* on color TV[26] and my uncle insisted on us seeing Queen's "Bohemian Rhapsody" video, which happened to be on. At the conclusion, he asked if we liked it. I was *horrified*; I had never seen anything like that before. My uncle, to my surprise—and that of my parents—admired it and thought it was ground-breaking. Now, over time, I have come

---

25. MKs can experience added isolation through fear of offending their parents' church (which might negatively influence their parents' funding) or undermining their parents' sense of call or missionary "image." There is also a hiding of your true feelings by projecting positivity when writing letters to your parents so that they will not worry about you. (This style of writing is learnt from reading your parents' prayer letters to supporters or in news articles they write for the mission's magazine! Such things are written, at least in part, to reinforce what *they think* their readers *want* to hear, i.e., replete with Christian jargon and a tone of triumphalism.)

26. I mistakenly interpreted having a *color* TV as meaning they were *very* wealthy. (*Top of the Pops* was a weekly music review of the top twenty singles in the UK; some acts were live and other groups/singers had promotional videos.)

to love it too, along with all the other Queen classics. Learning about "worldly" music, always pretty much taboo in my strict Pentecostal upbringing, was one huge adaptation for me. In slowly discovering my own expression of Christian faith, I was able to embrace and enjoy contemporary, secular music. I had years of catching up to do—including the Beatles.

Third, which items are medium-to-longer term depends on the degree of a person's TCK experience and the initial support they received—both mentioned earlier, along with the individual's temperament. In some cases, seeing a counselor is wise. Even so, some people may still have long-term vulnerabilities to certain elements on the list, e.g., a lower self-image, insecurity in relationships, depression, or heightened anxiety. Knowing that allows a person to be more aware of triggers and to implement and maintain guardrails, including good friends, which keep them from exaggerating stimuli or influences that have negative consequences. Actually, this commonsense advice applies to everyone.

Now here are some of the more positive aspects of the TCK experience:

1. Living abroad instills cross-cultural enrichment, including observational and language skills.
2. A larger worldview and open-mindedness; a sensitivity and an appreciation of the "other."
3. Knows how to fit in; adaptable—which doesn't necessarily mean compromising.
4. Has a sense of independence through living away from home and traveling alone (such as transcontinental air travel).
5. Witnessing firsthand faith lived out in practice.
6. Some MKs end up with a broader view of God.

The above systematic analysis of common TCK traits helped me better understand myself in context. It also made me realize that I wasn't an isolated and sometimes misunderstood oddity, but part of a much broader, international community of adult TCKs.

Consequently, I was able to revisit my past and process it better, sharing my learned insights with my wife and close friends.

The world has changed dramatically since the 1970s, obviously. We now live in a highly-mobile, global village—often, but not always, *by choice*. Air travel is far more common, and many young people get to experience other cultures firsthand (e.g., international students, exchange programs, gap years, summer vacations abroad). Related to this is the rise in immigration and increased numbers of refugees, both of which result in social challenges for children and adults alike.[27] One of the outcomes of such displacements is new terminology, such as *multicultural* and *multifaith*, which recognizes and tends to normalize or assimilate such experiences. Nevertheless, some Western countries are facing a crisis of their self-perceived national identity, resulting in increasing xenophobia and racism.[28] Since TCKs were, in a sense, pioneers or unwitting guinea pigs in social adaptation, I suggest the benefits of the above characteristics of adult TCKs have a wider relevance for today. Maybe our turbulent world needs the broader insights of adult TCKs . . .

Moving Forward

I attended three Hillcrest School reunions altogether, after which I decided not to attend any more. It was wonderful to know that those who were effectively "dead" to me, because they lived on a different continent, were actually still alive. Nevertheless, our lives had moved on. Regardless of how amazing our common past experiences had been (at least for the most part), we can never go back. We can only move forward. I now live in Canada, and although some Rock Haveners are only a three-and-a-half hours' drive away, I rarely visit them, but I take great comfort in knowing they are there. I have experienced a significant degree of emotional healing as a result of a much better understanding of

---

27. In the case of refugees, there is the added trauma linked to the reason they needed to leave their home country.

28. Such attitudes can be overt or covered by a thin veneer of respectability.

the enduring impact of being an MK/TCK/CCK. Put differently, I don't see myself as psychologically crippled by my upbringing. Even so, in addition to the positive TCK attributes identified above, there remains a lingering negative legacy; both are simply a part of who I am, even if the latter fades steadily over time. For example, having moved house, school, city, and country so many times I am left with itchy feet. Consequently, I have found it hard to put down deep roots, as after several years I begin to wonder if it's time to move on to a new job or location. That tendency for high mobility remained for several decades and I have had to curb that feeling for the sake of my family.[29]

I heard or read somewhere, "Don't pick at your scabs, it will slow down the body's healing process." What can be left in the end are physical scars, but they themselves are proof of the healing.[30] Whenever you see them, you are reminded of the trauma of the original injury, but there's no need to relive it. I suggest invisible emotional scars are similar. However, it seems to me that "inner" healing is only ever partial, sufficient for the present moment. We will likely need to address similar issues at later stages in life, as we experience new triggers that can bring up echoes of our past. With that in mind, regularly attending school reunions is *for me* an unnecessary reliving of those cycles of joy and loss. Nevertheless, I have *no regrets* for having been a missionary kid. It has broadened my horizons and shaped my life for the better. In my mind, the positives have far outweighed the negatives. My life has been profoundly enriched by my African experiences; I am so glad to have had them and wouldn't want to have missed them for the world.

---

29. It has been said that MKs/TCKs feel most at home in airports; that's a feeling I understand. My job as a university professor entailed a fair bit of international travel for research and conferences, so satisfying my itchy feet. Over the last fifteen years I have become far more settled in that regard and no longer feel the need to pack my suitcase once more.

30. Note, too, that a scar is a visible sign of healing or closure, but your body has *not* returned back to its pre-injury state. Too often we assume that healing means a return to normal, meaning things *as they used to be*. Clearly, that's not the case for a serious injury and the scar is an indelible reminder of a now past event.

Afterword

A MEMOIR BY DEFINITION is a *personal* retelling of past events. My recollections are therefore my own, and while I believe them to be a faithful account, they may not be entirely accurate as to what actually happened; others who shared those memories may recall things slightly differently. That is entirely normal and to be expected, especially after fifty years! My recollections have largely been triggered by my photographs and supplemented with factual details from letters, report cards, school yearbooks, and other publicly available documents. My reflections are my *interpretations* of some of those events and are obviously equally personal. Others may view things differently or put their own emphasis in another place, and that, too, is to be expected—particularly for those who experienced that time period as adults, such as teachers, house parents, and other missionaries. With that qualification, I hope that you have enjoyed reading these *Recollections and Reflections of a Missionary Kid's African Experiences* and have learned new insights.

Bibliography

Anonymous. "This World Is Not My Home." Hymnary, c. 1919. https://hymnary.org/text/this_world_is_not_my_home_im_just_a.
Boer, Jan Harm. *The Last of the Livingstones: H. Karl W. Kumm's Missiological Conception of Civilization*. Amsterdam: Free Reformed University, 1973. Revised 2014. http://socialtheology.com/docs/boer-paper-090073.pdf.
———. *Missionary Messengers of Liberation in a Colonial Context: A Case Study of the Sudan United Mission*. Amsterdam Studies in Theology 1. Amsterdam: Rodopi, 1979. https://www.socialtheology.com/docs/missionary-messengers-000079.pdf.
———. *Missions: Heralds of Capitalism or Christ?* Ibadan, Nigeria: DayStar, 1984. Revised 2014. https://www.socialtheology.com/docs/boer-missions-book.pdf.
———. "The Politico-Colonial Context of Missions in Northern Nigeria." *Calvin Theological Journal* 19 (1984) 167–91. https://www.socialtheology.com/docs/boer-paper-071583.pdf.
Boer, Jan Harm, and Frances A. Boer. *Every Square Inch: A Nigeria Missionary Memoir 1966–1996*. Ibadan, Nigeria: Bookcraft, 2022.
Boyd, Gregory A. *The Myth of a Christian Nation: How the Quest for Political Power Is Destroying the Church*. Grand Rapids: Zondervan, 2006.
Brand, Paul, with Philip Yancey. *Pain: The Gift Nobody Wants*. New York: HarperCollins, 1993.
Clarke, Brian, and Stuart Macdonald. *Leaving Christianity: Changing Allegiances in Canada Since 1945*. Advancing Studies in Religion 2. Montreal: McGill-Queen's University Press, 2017.
Cok, Ronald S. *Down Bush: A Boy's Life in Africa*. CreateSpace, 2016.
Crossman, Tanya. "What Is a Cross Cultural Kid (CCK)?" https://www.tanyacrossman.com/blog/what-is-a-cross-cultural-kid-cck.
Daly, Michael Wood. *God Doesn't Live Here Anymore*. Eugene, OR: Cascade, 2023.

BIBLIOGRAPHY

Dean, John W. *Conservatives Without Conscience*. New York: Viking Penguin, 2006.

Donovan, Vincent J. *Christianity Rediscovered*. Maryknoll, NY: Orbis, 2003.

Elusoji, Solomon. "Twelve Years of Terror: A Timeline of the Boko Haram Insurgency." Channels, July 24, 2021. https://www.channelstv.com/2021/07/24/twelve-years-of-terror-a-timeline-of-the-boko-haram-insurgency/.

Elyea, Dan. "Hillcrest School." *Simroots* 22:1 (2005). https://www.simroots.org/Documents/SR22-1_2005sp_no.pdf.

———. "Hillcrest School, Part 2." *Simroots* 22:2 (2005). https://www.simroots.org/Documents/SR22-2_2005fl_no.pdf.

Goitom, Hanibal. *Nigeria: Boko Haram; Report for the US Department of Justice*. Washington, DC: Law Library of Congress, 2014. https://www.justice.gov/sites/default/files/eoir/legacy/2014/07/28/2014-010945%20NG%20RPT.pdf.

Guinness, Os. *The Gravedigger File: Papers on the Subversion of the Modern Church*. Downers Grove, IL: InterVarsity, 1983.

Hall, Douglas John. *The End of Christendom and the Future of Christianity*. Eugene, OR: Wipf and Stock, 2002.

Hamilton, Jean. *The Lonely Lake: The Chad Story*. Sidcup, UK: SUM, 1973.

Kobo, Ousman Murzik. "'No Victor and No Vanquished'—Fifty Years After the Biafran War." Origins, January 2020. https://origins.osu.edu/milestones/nigerian-civil-war-biafra-anniversary.

Leone, Dario. "The Story of the Concorde Supersonic Airliner That Chased a Solar Eclipse and Set a World Record." Aviation Geek Club, Jan. 3, 2020. https://theaviationgeekclub.com/the-story-of-the-concorde-supersonic-airliner-that-chased-a-solar-eclipse-and-set-a-world-record/.

Mapping Militants Project. "Boko Haram." Last updated 2024. https://cisac.fsi.stanford.edu/mappingmilitants/profiles/boko-haram.

Maxwell, J. Lowry. *Half a Century of Grace: A Jubilee History of the Sudan United Mission*. Sidcup, UK: SUM, 1953. https://missiology.org.uk/pdf/e-books/maxwell_j-lowry/half-a-century-of-grace_maxwell.pdf.

#Memorias Situadas. "Biafran War Memories." 2016. https://www.cipdh.gob.ar/memorias-situadas/en/lugar-de-memoria/biafran-war-memories/.

Newbigin, Lesslie. *Foolishness to the Greeks: Gospel and Western Culture*. Grand Rapids: Eerdmans, 1986.

———. *The Gospel in a Pluralist Society*. Grand Rapids: Eerdmans, 1989.

———. *Proper Confidence: Faith, Doubt, and Certainty in Christian Discipleship*. Grand Rapids: Eerdmans, 1995.

Pham-Duc, Binh, et al. "The Lake Chad Hydrology Under Current Climate Change." *Scientific Reports* 10 (2020). https://doi.org/10.1038/s41598-020-62417-w.

Pinnock, Clark H. *Most Moved Mover: A Theology of God's Openness*. Grand Rapids: Baker, 2001.

Pollock, David C., and Ruth E. Van Reken. *The Third Culture Kid Experience: Growing Up Among Worlds*. Yarmouth, ME: Intercultural, 1999.

Rao, Joe. "One of the Longest Solar Eclipses on Earth Darkened the Sky 50 Years Ago. Here's How It Happened." Space.com, June 30, 2023. https://www.space.com/solar-eclipse-1973.

Reddish, Tim. *Does God Always Get What God Wants? An Exploration of God's Activity in a Suffering World*. Eugene, OR: Cascade, 2018.

Rekacewicz, Philippe. "Lake Chad: Almost Gone." GRID-Arendal, 2009. https://www.grida.no/resources/5593.

Sanders, John. *The God Who Risks: A Theology of Divine Providence*. 2nd ed. Downers Grove, IL: InterVarsity, 2007.

Simroots. "Resources for Cross-Cultural Workers and TCKs." https://www.simroots.org/Documents/Adult_TCK_Resources_for_web.pdf.

Smith, Carolyn D., ed. *Strangers at Home: Essays on the Effects of Living Overseas and Coming "Home" to a Strange Land*. Bayside, NY: Aletheia, 1996.

Smith, Gregory A., et al. *45% of Americans Say U.S. Should Be a "Christian Nation."* Washington, DC: Pew Research Center, 2022. https://www.pewresearch.org/wp-content/uploads/sites/20/2022/10/PF_2022.10.27_christian-nationalism_REPORT.pdf.

Solzhenitsyn, Aleksandr. *The Gulag Archipelago, 1918–1956: An Experiment in Literary Investigation, I–II*. Translated by Thomas P. Whitney. Vol. 1. New York: Harper & Row, 1973.

SUM. *The Lightbearer* 65:6. Sandbach, UK: Wright's, 1969.

———. *The Lightbearer* 72:2. Sandbach, UK: Wright's, 1976.

Tett, Mollie E. *The Road to Freedom: Sudan United Mission, 1904–1968*. Sidcup, UK: SUM, 1969.

Time and Date. "June 30, 1973—Total Solar Eclipse—Maiduguri, Borno, Nigeria (Yerwa)." https://www.timeanddate.com/eclipse/in/nigeria/maiduguri?iso=19730630.

Van Reken, Ruth E. *Letters Never Sent*. Indianapolis: Cook, 1988.

Wilkerson, David. *I've Given Up on Parents*. London: Hodder & Stoughton, 1969.

Wilkerson, David, with John and Elizabeth Sherrill. *The Cross and the Switchblade*. New York: Geis, 1963.

Wilson, Dorothy Clarke. *Ten Fingers for God*. Grand Rapids: Zondervan, 1989.

Wink, Walter. *The Powers That Be: Theology for a New Millennium*. New York: Doubleday, 1998.

About the Author

TIM REDDISH HAS A PhD in physics from Manchester, UK, and an MDiv from Knox College, Toronto. In late 2022 he retired from St. Andrew's Presbyterian Church, Amherstburg, Ontario, having been their minister for nearly five years. His previous career was as a physics professor at the Universities of Windsor, Ontario, and Newcastle upon Tyne, UK, researching in experimental atomic, molecular, and optical physics for twenty-five years. He spent his formative years in Nigeria and has a diverse church background—Assemblies of God, Baptist, Anglican, and Presbyterian. Tim and his family moved to Canada in 2002. His first wife, Anne, died of cancer in January 2011. His son, Philip, and his family now live in Edmonton and Tim is a grandfather of three. Tim remarried twelve-and-a-half years ago and enjoys being a stepdad to four young adults. He and his wife, Mary, live in Windsor. He loves reading theology and mystery/spy novels, watching British detective stories and period dramas, F1 racing, and photography. He is also the author of four other books, and coeditor of another.

Other Books by Tim Reddish

The Jesus I Didn't Know I Didn't Know
Reflections on the Identity of Jesus

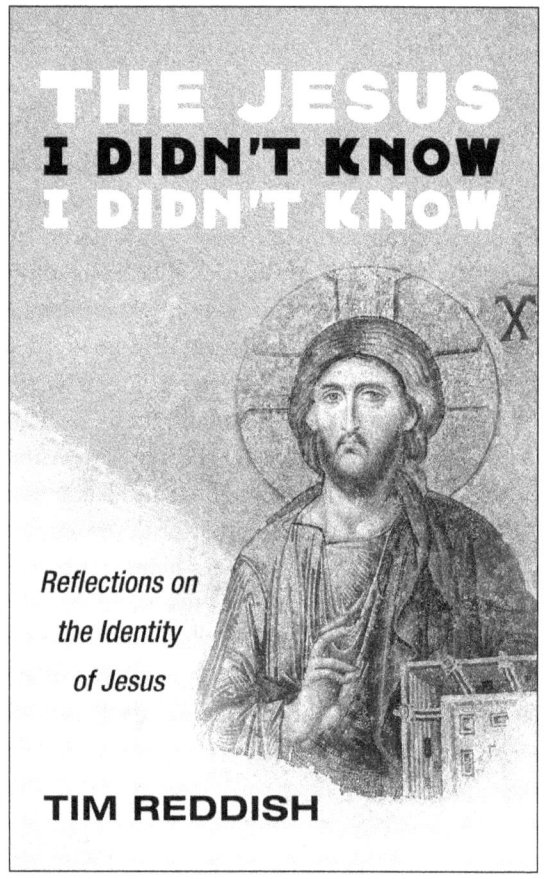

WIPF & STOCK · Eugene, Oregon

If you could draw together the best devotional writing and the best biblical scholarship and fuse them into a single book, then you would have *The Jesus I Didn't Know I Didn't Know*. Make no mistake you will not be able to read these words and remain unchanged. Some of the chapters will move you, others will challenge you, and some will just plain knock you out! It's a complete heart, mind, and soul workout—and I can't recommend it highly enough.

—**Rev. Dr. Nicholas Bundock**, Rector of St. James and Emmanuel Church, Manchester, UK.

Tim Reddish writes like a learned friend. With writing precision Tim navigates the space between learning and encouraging. I was persistently aware of the sense that I was listening to someone that cared about me; that he was unveiling for me previously unrealized, simple, but explosive ideas. Ideas with which I could both easily engage and understand. . . . Tim presents a truth, and then, rather than overwhelm a reader, takes an example and unpacks it in a way that is accessible. I think that newcomers to faith, and those long in the journey will benefit from reading this book.

—**Rev. Roland Hearn**, District Superintendent Australia North and West District of the Church of the Nazarene and the Coordinator for Ministry in Australia and New Zealand.

Does God Always Get What God Wants?
An Exploration of God's Activity in a Suffering World

Tim Reddish

 CASCADE *Books* • Eugene, Oregon

Tim Reddish, trained both in physics and theology, has a nimble mind, and this probing of the relationship between human suffering and God is deft and profound. But mainly this is a deeply personal book, one in which Reddish's own experience with loss and grief sends him farther along the path of faith. His journey takes him not to neatly crafted answers but instead to the cross of Jesus Christ. Readers of this book will learn much, and they will also be powerfully moved.

—**Thomas G. Long**, Bandy Emeritus Professor of Preaching, Candler School of Theology, Emory University, and author of *What Shall We Say? Evil, Suffering, and the Crisis of Faith.*

Drawing from Scripture, tradition, science, and his own very personal experience with tragedy, Tim Reddish offers readers a clear, comprehensive, and compelling response to the problem of evil—one that doesn't require us to accept that the horrendous suffering people often endure is part of God's grand plan but that nevertheless offers people great hope and comfort . . .

—**Gregory A. Boyd**, Senior Pastor of Woodland Hills Church, St. Paul, Minnesota, and author of *Is God to Blame?* and *Satan and the Problem of Evil.*

Science and Christianity
Foundations and Frameworks for
Moving Forward in Faith

WIPF & STOCK · Eugene, Oregon

The polarized positions, from within the church and from skeptics outside, are so loud and so effectively disseminated that it is often difficult for sensible, mediating positions to be heard. But I am encouraged that there are more and more such positions, including this straightforward defense of critical realism. Reddish's concluding challenge to "*Let Scripture be*" should be a helpful word in season for church audiences.

—**Mark Noll**, Francis A. McAnaney Professor of History at the University of Notre Dame, and author of *Jesus Christ and the Life of the Mind*.

Reddish engages Scripture faithfully and science with professional integrity. In this book readers will find a helpful guide to understanding not just the perennial flash points of science and Christianity, but the deeper issues that have conditioned the modern mind to be suspicious of finding common ground between them. Reddish shows not just that science and faith can get along, but that when each is understood properly, they enrich each other.

—**Jim Stump**, Senior Editor, *BioLogos*, and author of *Science and Christianity: An Introduction to the Issues*.

The Amish Farmer Who Hated L.A.
And 8 Other Modern-Day Allegories

In this book the delights of imagination meet timeless stories of Scripture. The outcome is the retelling of deep truths about both the human condition and God's remarkable grace. Tim Reddish has given us a whimsical and thought-provoking read that is also pure pleasure.

—**Rev. Dr. Judy Paulsen**, Professor of Evangelism, Wycliffe College, Toronto.

Tim Reddish writes to address difficult questions from interesting angles. His work feels fresh, contemporary, challenging, and thought-provoking—without departing from orthodox faith. This book helps us to reflect on our lives, the better to serve the One who gave us life.

—**Ven. Nick Barker**, Archdeacon of Auckland and Priest-in-Charge of Holy Trinity, Darlington, UK.

This collection of short stories warms the heart and provides insight into how God is at work through people today. The stories take biblical topics and situate them into contemporary cultural settings, and so help to open our eyes to their meaning for today. Tim Reddish takes on a number of interesting topics and handles them with grace.

—**Dr. John Sanders**, Professor of Religious Studies, Hendrix College, and author of *The God Who Risks*.

www.ingramcontent.com/pod-product-compliance
Lightning Source LLC
Chambersburg PA
CBHW071716040426
42446CB00011B/2093